PARTICIPATORY ACTION RESEARCH

QUALITATIVE RESEARCH METHODS

Series Editor

JOHN VAN MAANEN Massachusetts Institute of Technology

Associate Editors: Peter K. Manning, Northeastern University & Marc L. Miller, University of Washington Other volumes in this series listed on outside back cover

PARTICIPATORY ACTION RESEARCH

Alice McIntyre
Hellenic College

QUALITATIVE
RESEARCH
METHODS
SERIES
52

SAGE Publications
Los Angeles • London • New Delhi • Singapore

McIntyre, A. (2000). *Inner-city kids: Adolescents confront life and violence in an urban community.* Selections reprinted with the permission of New York University Press.

McIntyre, A. (2004). *Women in Belfast: How violence shapes identity.* Selections reproduced with permission of Greenwood Publishing Group, Inc., Westport, CT.

For information:

Sage Publications, Inc.
2455 Teller Road
Thousand Oaks, California 91320
E-mail: order@sagepub.com

Sage Publications India Pvt. Ltd.
B 1/I 1 Mohan Cooperative
  Industrial Area
Mathura Road, New Delhi 110 044
India

Sage Publications Ltd.
1 Oliver's Yard
55 City Road
London EC1Y 1SP
United Kingdom

Sage Publications Asia-Pacific Pte. Ltd.
33 Pekin Street #02-01
Far East Square
Singapore 048763

Printed in the United States of America

Library of Congress Cataloging-in-Publication Data

McIntyre, Alice, 1956-
Participatory action research / Alice McIntyre.
    p. cm. — (Qualitative research methods; 52)
Includes bibliographical references and index.
ISBN 978-1-4129-5366-5 (pbk.)
    1. Social sciences—Research. 2. Action research. 3. Communities—Research.
4. Social participation. 5. Group problem solving. I. Title.

H62.M3363 2008
300.72—dc22   2007033164

This book is printed on acid-free paper.

07 08 09 10 11   10 9 8 7 6 5 4 3 2 1

Acquisitions Editor:	Vicki Knight
Associate Editor:	Sean Connelly
Editorial Assistant:	Lauren Habib
Production Editor:	Diane S. Foster
Copy Editor:	Tony Moore
Typesetter:	C&M Digitals (P) Ltd.
Proofreader:	Caryne Brown
Marketing Manager:	Stephanie Adams
Cover Designer:	Candice Harman

To Brinton Lykes, who showed me the extent to which PAR could effect change, and to all those who have kept me engaged in life, scholarship, research, teaching, and the pursuit of justice and fair play, many thanks. Many thanks also go to Margo Crouppen, Lisa Cuevas Shaw, Vicki Knight, and the other people at Sage for saying yes. Tony, thanks for your keen eyes. Michelle, your designs are, as my friends in Belfast would say, "dead on!" To the reviewers: Thank you for taking the time to review this work and for providing me with valuable comments and questions.
Above all, thank you to the participants of the PAR projects described herein. I deeply appreciate your willingness to accompany me on the messy, challenging, humorous, and creative road of PAR.

Contents

Introduction

Many years ago, when I was frustrated by one of the very humanizing moments of a participatory action research (PAR) project, I thought of something that I had heard the previous year at an academic conference: "When you get to the crossroads, take it." Since then, I have stood at the crossroads in PAR projects multiple times—and the advice still stands: When I get to the crossroads, I take it. In other words, when I am in doubt about what to do, I do something. The "somethings" I have done in the context of PAR have humbled, encouraged, disappointed, surprised, and reassured me. They have also reminded me of the necessity of PAR within the social sciences and the need for researchers from across a number of disciplines to participate *with* people in improving and understanding the world by changing it (McTaggart, 1991).

In this book, I describe how participants in two different PAR projects engaged in collaborative processes aimed at improving and understanding their worlds in order to change them. I do so by focusing on three characteristics of PAR: the active participation of researchers and participants in the co-construction of knowledge; the promotion of self- and critical awareness that leads to individual, collective, and/or social change; and the building of alliances between researchers and participants in the planning, implementation, and dissemination of the research process. I describe how the participants of both projects became the primary actors in the research process, enhancing their understanding and knowledge of issues through individual and collective reflection and investigation. I then explore how the participants took action to improve their conditions, clarify information to outside communities, and gain a better understanding of the external circumstances that structure their lives.

One of the projects I highlight is a 3-year PAR project I engaged in with a group of adolescents of color living in an inner-city community in the Northeast region of the United States. Together, we explored how these adolescents experience the multiple forms of violence that characterize their lives (McIntyre, 2000). The second PAR project discussed in this book reveals how a group of women living in Belfast, the North of Ireland, participated in a project aimed at bringing to light the gendered violence that occurred during that country's 35-year war (McIntyre, 2004).[1] By engaging in PAR processes, the women and the young people articulated how violence is produced, reproduced, and experienced in their lives. Out of those articulations, both groups implemented action plans that addressed issues salient to them, both individually and collectively. I briefly describe those projects below.

PAR: CONSTRUCTING MEANING AND ENACTING CHANGE WITH URBAN YOUTH

From 1997 to 2000, I engaged in a PAR project at the Blair Elementary and Middle School,[2] an inner-city public school in Bridgeport, Connecticut. Although located in one of the wealthiest counties in the United States, Bridgeport has a disproportionate share of the problems that affect many urban communities throughout the country—for example, high criminal activity, unemployment and low-wage jobs, underresourced schools, and racial isolation.

In 1997, I was introduced to Mrs. Leslie, a sixth-grade teacher at the Blair School. She invited me to present my idea about a PAR project to her 24 African American, Jamaican, Puerto Rican, Dominican, and Haitian students (12 boys and 12 girls). I told the young people a little bit about myself: my experiences growing up and teaching in Boston schools, my journey from classroom teaching to teaching in a university, and my desire to collaborate with them in exploring what it meant for them to live in a Bridgeport community. After a lively discussion about how we would engage that exploration, the young people decided to participate in the project.

Over a 3-year period, a group of graduate students from the university where I worked, a shifting population of young adolescents, and I met together once a week for an average of an hour and a half per group session. Together, we participated in a range of project-related activities aimed at furthering the young people's goal of informing their community about the effects of violence on themselves, their schools, and their environment (see, McIntyre, 2000, for a detailed description of the PAR project).

WOMEN RESEARCHING THEIR LIVES: PAR IN BELFAST, THE NORTH OF IRELAND

I first visited Belfast in 1996 and made contact with a number of women, local community workers, teachers, children, parents, and caregivers. I returned to Belfast a number of times over the next 2 years to work with children and youth in a local Irish school as well as in a local youth center.

During my years working with the young people, I lived with a family in the Monument Road community—where both the school and the youth center are located.[3] By living with and among Monument Road residents, participating in a host of community activities, and facilitating a project with a group of children in the community, I gained a better understanding of what life is like for the people living there. During that time, I also developed friendships with a group of women who invited me to collaborate with them in designing a project aimed at exploring issues that affect them as mothers, daughters, wives, partners, caregivers, and the primary stakeholders in community life.

I formulated a letter that the women disseminated to other women in the community inviting them to participate in the project. In the letter, I introduced myself and described my/our ideas for a project that would specifically address issues of concern to the women living in the Monument Road community. The women informed me that they would contact me in the United States with the names of the women who elected to participate. We would then draft a schedule and a framework for how the project would proceed. When the project began, the nine women that ultimately participated ranged in age from 24 to 40. Some of them are married; others divorced or single; some have children; others do not; some are employed; others are not working outside the home (see McIntyre, 2004).

For 2 years, the women engaged in informative, reflective, and critical dialogue about their experiences living in the Monument Road community. By engaging in that dialogue and participating in a wide range of consciousness-raising activities, the women constructed new ways of viewing their lives and new strategies for communicating their experiences to others.

The stories of how a group of young urban adolescents of color living in the United States and a group of Irish working-class women living in Belfast, the North of Ireland, move from a place of dialoguing about issues that are of concern to them to a place where they take action on those issues was mediated by the very humanness that characterizes PAR projects. There were complications, confusion, and a host of distractions. There were moments of connection, revelation, and genuine collaboration. There were moments of enlightenment, resignation, and all kinds of moments in between.

Traditional methods of social science research would not have contained the push and pull of conflicting and competing moments, agendas, and perspectives that were inherent in the participatory processes described herein. Nor would conventional research paradigms provide a framework for addressing the researcher–participant relationship, the codeveloping of the research process, and the positioning of consciousness-raising and affecting change within the overall research experience.

Participatory action research *does* provide opportunities for codeveloping processes *with* people rather than *for* people. Its emphasis on people's lived experiences, individual and social change, the coconstruction of knowledge, and "the notion of action as a legitimate mode of knowing, thereby taking the realm of knowledge into the field of practice" (Tandon, 1996, p. 21) has the potential to create public spaces where researchers and participants can reshape their understanding of how political, educational, social, economic, and familial contexts mediate people's lives.

A NOTE ABOUT TERMINOLOGY

The people involved in PAR projects are defined in a host of different ways. The definitions practitioners and participants use are always in flux and oftentimes contested. That is because practitioners of PAR reject the kind of dualisms that characterize traditional social science research and therefore make every effort to equalize the relationships that exist in PAR projects. As McTaggart (2001) argues, the distinction between academics and participants of PAR projects must not be taken to imply that "theory reside[s] in one place and its implementation in another. Such a view is the antithesis of the commitment of participatory action research that seeks the development of theoretically informed practice for all parties involved" (p. 266).

In the case of the two projects described here, I invited the young people and the women to decide how we would identify ourselves in any writings or presentations that resulted from our work together. I explained the various terms that were used in the literature related to participatory action research. I also informed them that we could generate our own terminology that was particular to our respective projects.

Both groups recognized that, as Tonesha, one of the young people, said, "We're all in this together." Yet they also recognized that we all had different roles and responsibilities as researchers, participants, and collaborators in a PAR process. The young people agreed that we needed to be clear to each other and to our respective audiences (e.g., faculty members, community groups, school-aged students, and parents and caregivers) about what those roles and responsibilities were. As Monique stated, "You're like the researcher, Dr. Mac, and we're the ones who are researching, too, but you have to show us how to do that. But you can participate, too, 'cause we all have to participate."

The women in Belfast felt similarly. Although they agreed that we were all participants in a collaborative process, they also believed that we needed to be clear about our respective roles within the project. As Tricia stated,

There's a difference between you and us, Alice. You're a researcher first. Then a person who participates in the project. We're the community, the ones who are here, who participate in everything. We're learning through this project how to do research. But we're participants first and then researchers. (November 1, 2001)

Based on the discussions I engaged in with the young people and the women, and to provide clarity to the reader, I use the terms researcher and practitioner to describe me and my role in the projects. The university-based team consists of the graduate students who participated in the Bridgeport project. I include myself as a member of that team. I use the term participant to describe the young people who participated in the Bridgeport project and the women who participated in the Belfast project. Since PAR creates spaces where all those involved have a part to play in reaching consensus about project-related issues, I include myself as a participant in both projects.

A Disclaimer

The Publication Manual of the American Psychological Association (2001) states that "Racial and ethnic groups are designated by proper nouns and are capitalized. Therefore, use *Black* and *White* instead of *black* and *white* (colors to refer to other human groups currently are considered pejorative and should not be used)" (p. 68).

I argue that many people in the United States have beliefs about race that have been shaped and influenced by entrenched beliefs about the dominance of whites and the subjugation of people of color. Thus, if I were in the position to decide how to refer to racial groups within this book, I would use the uppercase *B* for *Black* and the lowercase *w* for *white*, because, as Harris (1993) states, both have "a particular political history. Although 'white' and 'Black' have been defined oppositionally, they are not functional opposites. 'White' has incorporated Black subordination; 'Black' is not based on domination . . . 'Black' is naming that is part of the counter-hegemonic practice" (p. 1710). In keeping with Harris's position, I would also use the uppercase *C* for *people of Color*.

OUTLINE OF THE BOOK

The book is organized into five chapters. Chapter One introduces PAR, tracing its roots from Latin America, Africa, and other parts of the world to Canada and the United States. In addition, I describe how PAR offers a multidimensional approach to research that intentionally integrates participants' life experiences into the research process. Too often, cultural, religious, familial, and community beliefs, as well as related practices that are particular to specific groups of people, are overlooked within research projects directed at marginalized communities. The two projects presented in this book are exceptions. Both communities are constituted by diverse linguistic, cultural, ethnic, religious, gendered, and racial practices. Thus, these practices needed to be explored, critiqued, and utilized. Participatory action research is *one* research approach that has the capacity to address those varied practices. Finally, I discuss the ethical issues that are generated in PAR—issues that need to be mutually addressed by practitioners and participants throughout the research process.

In Chapter Two, I focus on the meaning of "participation" in PAR projects. I provide an overview of the process by which the young people in Bridgeport and the women in Belfast came to understand how their individual and collective participation in PAR informed both processes. As important, both groups of participants realized that participation is not fixed. Rather, it is a fluid process that is dependent on an individual's decision to participate in a research process, as well as an individual's ability to be present to the multifaceted aspects of a PAR project. Both the young people and the women brought different sets of skills, talents, strengths, desires, and interests to the table—all of which needed to be taken into account when decisions were made about where to go, what to do, and how to do it.

In Chapter Three, I move from foregrounding "participation" to highlighting the meanings of "action" and "change" within PAR processes. The book shifts from exploring how the young people and the women generated knowledge to demonstrating how both groups formulated action plans to address the information they gathered. I also examine the challenges both groups of participants faced in developing said action plans. Some of the challenges that were generated in terms of what actions the young people took in their project had to do with age, access to resources, and the ability to implement particular actions. For example, the participants wanted to organize a citywide cleanup event that required more time, energy, and human power than we had at our disposal. Therefore, the young people reconsidered their original idea and decided to limit their actions to their own neighborhood. In so doing, they acted in accordance with the aims of the project while exhibiting a keen understanding of their limitations.

The challenges that were generated in terms of the actions the women in Belfast engaged in had more to do with living most of their lives in the context of war—a context that, for many of the women, was and is marked by various forms of silence. Sometimes the women felt, as Patricia stated, "free to talk about stuff we've never talked about really, well, not in a group like this." Other times, the women's desire to talk with one another, and with me, was overshadowed by a desire to remain silent about a number of events that have informed and influenced the ways they engage the world.

The women's individual and collective tugs-of-war about what to say, what not to say, and how to act on the information that was generated in the group sessions reveals the complexities that accompany self- and collective revelations within PAR processes. In addition, the women's struggles with how to act on the knowledge gleaned from the research process reminds practitioners of PAR to attend to participants' fears and anxieties when deciding how to make visible what is sometimes left invisible in social science research.

In Chapters Two and Three, I also describe how the participants in both projects engaged in photovoice (Wang, 1999)—a methodology that enabled both groups to use cameras to record aspects of their daily lives from their own perspectives. In addition, photovoice provided opportunities for the young people and the women to focus on aspects of their lives and communities that they are proud of, as well as the ones about which they have the greatest concerns (see Ewald, 2001; Lykes, 2001; McIntyre, 2000, 2004; and Wang, Wu, Zhan, & Carovano, 1998, for further discussions of photovoice).

In Chapter Four, I discuss what constitutes "research" in participatory action research. I do so by discussing how the participation of the young people and the women in their respective projects illuminates salient aspects of research: inquiry, investigation, analysis, and dissemination of knowledge. In both projects, the groups engaged in inquiry-based activities that generated multiple forms of knowledge. Through photography, painting, collages, and other forms of gathering knowledge, the young people and the women collected information about themselves and their communities. Out of that knowledge, they uncovered themes about their lives that informed how they crafted the action phases of their projects.

In addition, the participant groups became active decision makers in what stories and events would be revealed to outside audiences. For the young people, they made multiple decisions about what information to include in presentations to government officials, to faculty and students at two universities, to the members of the Blair School community, and to the media. The participants also made multiple decisions in the design of a photo-text book and in the creation of a group they formed called "One STEP," the Save The Earth Program (see One STEP Group, McIntyre, & McKeirnan, 2000). The women of Belfast made decisions about what information to reveal to outside communities as it pertained to the photo-text exhibit they designed and displayed at the 2003 West Belfast Festival in the North of Ireland.

I also invited both groups of participants—in different ways, given their ages and their unfamiliarity with academic publishing—to coauthor manuscripts with me, as well as to review articles, chapters of books, and professional presentations that I was in the process of writing. I asked both participant groups to inform me if they agreed with my interpretations of certain events and/or if they understood the ways in which I formulated links between various aspects of the project.

The women were reluctant to coauthor a publication with me. As Lucy stated, "We promise we'll read the stuff, Alice. But we're not writin' with ya. We'll make ya cups of tea, feed ya every night, but no, we're not writin' anythin' with ya." The young people, on other hand, were eager to communicate their work to others. Yet instead of co-authoring a journal article with me, they chose to coauthor various presentations they gave to outside communities, as well as to codesign and cowrite the previously noted One STEP photo-text book.

Notwithstanding the strategies I/we employed so that both groups of participants could collaborate in the analysis and dissemination of the data I used for academic-related work, I was the sole framer of those writings.

In the final chapter, I revisit the ethical issues that arise in PAR projects. In addition, I discuss the implications of PAR to effect individual and collective change. I suggest that PAR can bring about new ways of thinking about what life is like for various groups of people throughout the world—ways of thinking that will assist those groups in developing strategies for individual and collective well-being. I also encourage educators, community activists, psychologists, and researchers to act on the insights gleaned from PAR and take responsibility for initiating effective and transformative ways to pursue action-based research with participating communities.

CONCLUDING REFLECTIONS

Through my experiences as a practitioner of PAR in the United States and in Belfast, the North of Ireland, I have learned to focus on the importance of context in exploring, explaining, and acting on community issues. In addition, I have learned the importance of cocreating spaces with marginalized groups where they can speak their stories into life; where they "are free to choose—authentically and for themselves, individually, and in the context of mutual participation" (Kemmis & McTaggart, 2005, p. 577)—how to take actions that will improve their current situations.

Engaging in PAR with the women in Belfast and the young people in Bridgeport—both of whom have been socially excluded, economically disadvantaged, and institutionally marginalized in their respective countries— was one way to both accompany people as they worked for change and to more effectively address their needs through collaborative efforts. That does not mean that PAR is a panacea for the multiple issues that mediate life for so many groups worldwide. As with other forms of research, there are ambiguities, complications, and unexpected challenges. Yet those challenges do not have to derail the PAR process. Rather, they can be used to reconstitute how we "do research." As a result of that reconstitution, practitioners of PAR can provide opportunities for participants to strengthen their awareness about their individual and collective skills, resources, and abilities to build communities of inquiry and change.

Given the diversity of perspectives, the variety of methods, the different research approaches, the wide range of objectives, and the underlying principles that underscore PAR, it appears unreasonable to think that there will ever be a *fully* realized PAR project. Yet as far as I can tell, that is not the overarching reason that practitioners and participants engage in participatory action research. Rather, I suggest it is because they believe in PAR's potential to explain and interpret reality so as to change it.

Lincoln and Goulet (1998) suggest that, "We have been doing the right work but sometimes we are not certain that we are doing the work right" (p. 229). This book explores one way of engaging in the "right work" while recognizing that doing the "work right" is an ongoing, humanizing process that we learn as we go.

NOTES

1. The recent war in the North of Ireland, often referred to as the "Troubles," began with the British invasion of Ireland and the partition of Ireland in 1921 into 26 free counties in the South and 6 British-governed counties in the North. The launch of the recent Troubles occurred in 1968

when the drive for civil rights came to the fore in the North of Ireland. Over the next 35 years, over 3,500 people were killed in the Troubles.

2. In both projects, many of the names of people, places, and things have been changed. Some of the women chose to use their birth names. The majority of the women, and all of the young people, chose pseudonyms, which were used throughout the project.

3. People living in the Monument Road community suffered greatly during the war. Over 50 residents of Monument Road were murdered, and many more were injured, imprisoned, or forced to leave the area.

1

PARTICIPATORY ACTION RESEARCH

Practitioners of PAR engage in a variety of research projects, in a variety of contexts, using a wide range of research practices that are related to an equally wide range of political ideologies. Yet there are underlying tenets that are specific to the field of PAR and that inform the majority of PAR projects: (a) a collective commitment to investigate an issue or problem, (b) a desire to engage in self- and collective reflection to gain clarity about the issue under investigation, (c) a joint decision to engage in individual and/or collective action that leads to a useful solution that benefits the people involved, and (d) the building of alliances between researchers and participants in the planning, implementation, and dissemination of the research process.

These aims are achieved through a cyclical process of exploration, knowledge construction, and action at different moments throughout the research process. As participants engage in PAR, they simultaneously address integral aspects of the research process—for example, the question of who benefits from a PAR project; what constitutes data; how will decision making be implemented; and how, and to whom, will the information generated within the PAR project be disseminated? As the PAR process evolves, these and other questions are re-problematized in the light of critical reflection and dialogue between and among participating actors. It is by actively engaging in critical dialogue and collective reflection that the participants of PAR recognize that they have a stake in the overall project. Thus, PAR becomes a living dialectical process, changing the researcher, the participants, and the situations in which they act (McTaggart, 1997a).

The originators of the principles, methodologies, epistemologies, and characterizations that inform PAR projects are worldwide and span many decades. In the late 1970s and 1980s, for example, Tandon (1981) and Kanhare (1980) initiated PAR projects in India that addressed adult education and women's development, respectively. In Columbia, Fals-Borda (1985, 1987) and his colleagues engaged in PAR projects aimed at increasing adult literacy. In neighboring Peru, de Wit and Gianotten (1980)

1

participated in a training program for rural farmers. In Chile, Vio Grossi (1982) worked with local communities to address agrarian reform. Swantz (1982) and Mbilinyi (1982) engaged in PAR processes to improve education for peasant women and other residents of Tanzania. In that same country, Mduma (1982) participated in a PAR project with local Tanzanians to develop agricultural technology.

Elsewhere in the world, Einar Thorsrud engaged in a PAR process that restructured work relations within the shipbuilding industry in Europe (Walton & Gaffney, 1989). In Canada, Jackson and McKay (1982) engaged with local people to improve water sanitation practices in Big Trout Lake. Hall (1977) addressed adult education in a variety of contexts in the United States, and in New Mexico, Maguire (1987) participated in a PAR project addressing male-to-female violence. At the Highlander Research and Education Center in Tennessee, Gaventa and Horton (1981) developed participatory strategies of reflection, action, and social change with various groups of people addressing a host of social and community issues.

Since then, many of the above researchers, as well as their counterparts in different regions of the globe, have increased the visibility of participatory action research. Similarly, they have re-demonstrated the wide range of issues that can be explored and acted upon in PAR, as well as the variety of contexts where PAR can be conducted. Greenwood and González accompanied industrial cooperatives in the Spanish Basque country as they learned research skills to organize and sustain the cooperatives' goals (Greenwood, Whyte, & Harkavy, 1993). Maglajlic (2004) engaged in PAR with university-based teams to develop strategies for the prevention of HIV/AIDS in Bosnia and Herzegovina. In Hong Kong, Siu and Kwok (2004) carried out a PAR project to generate strategies for improving integrated services for children and youth. In South Africa, Marincowitz (2003) engaged in a PAR project aimed at improving primary care for terminally ill patients. In Guatemala, Lykes (1997, 2001) addressed mental health in the context of state-sponsored violence. In the United States, McIntyre (1997) explored the meaning of whiteness with White teachers, and Brydon-Miller (1993) engaged in a PAR project with disabled persons advocating rights for the disabled. Fine and her colleagues (2003) collaborated in a PAR project with women inmates documenting the effects of prison-based college programs on current and postrelease prisoners.

A closer reading of the above projects, as well as a review of many others not listed here, reveals the context-specificity of participatory action research. Owing to that specificity, there is no fixed formula for designing, practicing, and implementing PAR projects. Nor is there one overriding theoretical framework that underpins PAR processes. Rather, there is malleability in how PAR processes are framed and carried out. In part, that is owing to the fact that practitioners of PAR, some of whom are community insiders and others who come from outside the community, draw from a variety of theoretical and ideological perspectives that inform their practice. Some researchers borrow from Marx's position that local people need to engage in critical reflection about the structural power of dominant classes in order to take action against oppression. Similarly, Gramsci's participation in class struggles and his belief that economic and self- and collective actualization can alleviate the uneven distribution of power in society have contributed to the belief among practitioners of PAR that people themselves are, and can be, catalysts for change (Hall, 1981).

Critical theory has also contributed to PAR since it suggests that researchers attend to how power in social, political, cultural, and economic contexts informs the ways in which people act in everyday situations (Collins, 1998; Kemmis, 2001). In addition, Bell (2001) argues that race must not be overlooked in research projects since the projects themselves are embedded in the theories and research practices that inform them— theories and practices that are themselves mediated by race.

Another major influence in the field of PAR is the work of the Brazilian adult educator Paulo Freire (1970, 1973, 1985). Freire's theory of conscientization, his belief in critical reflection as essential for individual and social change, and his commitment to the democratic dialectical unification of theory and practice have contributed significantly to the field of participatory action research. Similarly, Freire's development of counterhegemonic approaches to knowledge construction within oppressed communities has informed many of the strategies practitioners use in PAR projects.

As important, feminism has been a key contributor to the scholarship of participatory action research. Feminist theories (see, e.g., hooks, 2000; Collins, 1998; Morawski, 1994; Reinharz, 1992; Stewart, 1994; Wilkinson, 1996) have enhanced the field of PAR with perspectives that have evolved out of a refusal to accept theory, research, and ethical perspectives that ignore, devalue, and erase women's lives, experiences, and contributions to social science research. Beginning in the 1980s, Kanhare (1980), Lykes (1989), Maguire (1987), Mbilinyi (1982), Swantz, (1982), and Wadsworth (1984) demonstrated and articulated how feminist PAR could be implemented across a variety of contexts. They, and other researchers, continue that tradition today by providing clear frameworks about how feminist-infused PAR projects are "[m]aking the invisible visible, bringing the margin to the center, rendering the trivial important, [and] putting the spotlight on women as competent actors" (Reinharz, 1992, p. 248) in the life of the everyday (see, e.g., Brydon-Miller, Maguire, & McIntyre, 2004; Chataway, 1997; Chrisp, 2004; Fine et al., 2003; Greenwood, 2004; Lewis, 2001; Lykes, 2001; Maguire, 2004; McIntyre, 2000, 2004; Wadsworth, 2001). There is also a cross-fertilization of research traditions that characterize PAR, each having distinct geohistorical roots. Rapid rural appraisal (Mikkelsen 2001), critical action research (Kemmis & McTaggart, 2005), community-based participatory research (Minkler & Wallerstein, 2003), and participatory community research (Jason, Keys, Suarez-Balcazar, Taylor, & Davis, 2004) are all variants of PAR that traditionally focus on systemic investigations that lead to a reconfiguration of power structures, however those structures are organized in a particular community.

Some practitioners of PAR follow the tradition of action research—a research approach developed by Kurt Lewin in the 1940s that focuses on group dynamics and the belief that as people examine their realities, they will organize themselves to improve their conditions (McTaggart, 1991). The Tavistock Institute of Human Relations in London and the Work Research Institute in Oslo expanded Lewin's work exploring the notion of team building as an essential factor in improving organizational behavior and structure (Boog, 2003). In addition, variants of action research like co-operative inquiry (Heron,1988; Reason & Rowan, 1981) and action science (Argyris & Schön, 1989) have contributed to a better understanding of the relationship between theory building and processes of change within organizations and local communities.

Variants of PAR also exist within educational settings. Action research (Atweh, Kemmis, & Weeks, 1998; Elliott, 1991; Greenwood & Levin, 1998; Hollingsworth, 1997; Noffke & Somekh, 2005; and Zeichner, 2001), teacher research (Burnaford, Fischer, & Hobson, 2001; Cochran-Smith & Lytle, 1993; Mills, 2006; and Kincheloe, 2003), reflective practice-research (Evans, 2002; McDonald, 1992; and Schön, 1983), and community service-learning (Kay, 2003; Wade & Anderson, 1996; and Zeichner & Melnick, 1996) have contributed significantly to the development of more democratic teaching practices that are linked to students' and teachers' everyday lives.

To varying degrees, practitioners of the various research approaches listed above have underlying epistemological, methodological, and ideological differences. Similarly, they have different visions of social research, of the scientific method, and of the political and ethical commitments associated with different research approaches (Greenwood, Whyte, & Harkavy, 1993). For example, many action researchers are trained in management and organizational theory, where the emphasis is on individual and interpersonal levels of action and analysis (Brown & Tandon, 1983). On the other hand, many practitioners of community-based PAR are trained in community development, sociology, education, and political science, where the focus is on communities and social structures (Khanlou & Peter, 2005). The latter approach includes an emphasis on equity, oppression, and access to resources for research participants—factors that are not always present in other forms of action-based research.

Although it is important to highlight the particularities that exist between and among participatory, action-based research approaches, it is unwise to overemphasize their similarities and differences. As Brown (1982) suggests, "Similarities provide a foundation for communication and trust; differences offer possibilities for mutual learning and development" (p. 206). When explored, addressed, and critiqued, both the similarities and differences, as well as the gray areas in between, benefit the field of PAR, assisting practitioners in developing authentic and effective strategies for collaborating with people in improving their lives, effecting social change, and reconstituting the meaning and value of knowledge.

In this book, I use the term PAR to describe an approach to exploring the processes by which participants engage in collaborative, action-based projects that reflect their knowledge and mobilize their desires (Vio Grossi, 1980). I base my approach on the combined beliefs of Paulo Freire and feminist practitioners of PAR—an approach characterized by the active participation of researchers and participants in the coconstruction of knowledge; the promotion of self- and critical awareness that leads to individual, collective, and/or social change; and an emphasis on a colearning process where researchers and participants plan, implement, and establish a process for disseminating information gathered in the research project.

PAR: A BRAIDED PROCESS OF EXPLORATION, REFLECTION, AND ACTION

In addition to the traditions and ideologies that frame and contextualize a PAR project, each project is tailored to the desires of the research participants. Out of those desires, participants decide to act on particular topics that are generated in the PAR process. Participant-generated actions can range from changing public policy, to making recommendations to government agencies, to making informal changes in the community that benefit the people living there, to organizing a local event, to simply increasing awareness about an issue native to a particular locale. Ultimately, the actions that participants decide to take regarding their current circumstances are the result of the questions they pose, examine, and address within the overall research process.

The two projects discussed in this book were framed by initial questions that moved us along in various directions. Those directions provided opportunities for us to develop new ways of thinking about the issues raised in the group sessions. In addition, each new direction resulted in new ideas for how to address specific issues that warranted the participants' attention.

The initial questions that framed the projects led to other questions that emerged as the research processes evolved. Those questions then became points of entry into further reflection and dialogue that again led to new and different ways of perceiving the issues that were generated in both groups. Sometimes, the insight gained from reflection and dialogue prompted the participants to develop a plan of action. Other times, the participants reflected on a certain issue, discussed various perspectives about it, and ultimately decided that the item under discussion was not worth their time or attention.

This process of questioning, reflecting, dialoguing, and decision making resists linearity. Instead, PAR is a recursive process that involves a spiral of adaptable steps that include the following:

- Questioning a particular issue
- Reflecting upon and investigating the issue
- Developing an action plan
- Implementing and refining said plan

Figure 1.1 represents how various aspects of the PAR process are fluidly braided within one another in a spiral of reflection, investigation, and action. In the projects described herein, these steps were also linked to a set of activities (e.g., painting, sculpting, storytelling, collage-making, and photography) in which each group of participants engaged. Those activities, in turn, became entry points into yet more questions, more opportunities for reflecting and investigating issues, and more ideas about how to implement action plans that benefited those involved.

In the following chapters, I illustrate how the young people in Bridgeport and the women in Belfast engaged in the recursive process of participatory action research. Their experiences reveal the richness, complexity, and divergent perspectives that existed among them all. Similarly, their experiences demonstrate how participating in processes of critical scrutiny can result in thoughtful actions that reflect participants' interests and goals.

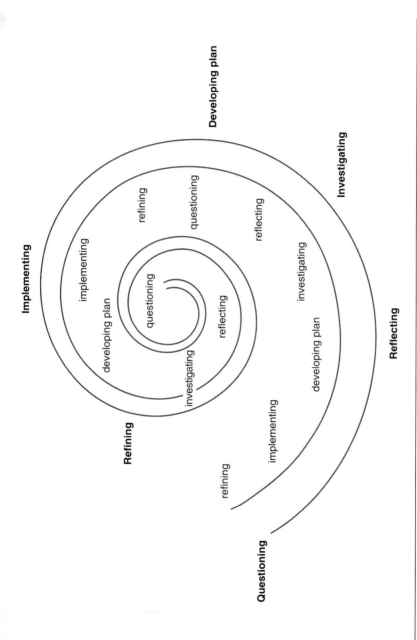

Figure 1.1   The Recursive Process of PAR

ACADEMIC RESEARCHERS AND LOCAL
PARTICIPANTS WITHIN PAR

A recurring question in PAR is whether a researcher needs to be requested as a resource by a community or group, or whether a researcher can approach a particular group inviting them to explore a particular issue (McIntyre, 2000). In many cases, the latter experience is the norm, particularly when the researcher is a college/university student or faculty member.

In both the Bridgeport and Belfast projects, I entered the sites as both a practitioner of PAR and an academic—a situation that raises a set of challenges that differ from those generated in PAR projects facilitated by persons unrelated to the academy. As I write elsewhere, there are distinctive challenges that emerge out of and through actual PAR experiences when they are linked to institutions of higher education (McIntyre, 1997; 2000). How academics who are also practitioners of PAR engage those challenges is dependent on the type of institution where they work, the positions they hold, and the multiple identities they carry. It is my experience that academics who engage in PAR need to make decisions about how they negotiate their respective roles in the academy and in the communities where they engage in PAR with caution and common sense. It also helps to hold the belief that, in their own ways, in their own time, and in the contexts in which they live and work, academic practitioners of PAR can shift the perception of the academy as an exclusive space for thinking and theorizing, to a site for collaborative experiences with local, national, and global communities.

Learning to Listen and Listening to Learn

An integral factor in how I negotiate my role as an academic practitioner of PAR in the communities in which I work is engaging in reflexivity, which I define as a dialectical process that occurs within the context of the social relationships that exist between research practitioners and participants (see, e.g., Chataway, 2001; Fine, 1994; Lykes, 1989; McIntyre & Lykes, 2004; Morawaski, 1994; Stewart, 1994). Reflexivity provides me with the opportunity to attend to how my personal biography informs my ability to listen, question, synthesize, analyze, and interpret knowledge throughout the PAR process.

In the Bridgeport project, it was essential for me to remember that the participants were 12- and 13-year-old inner-city adolescents of color, participating in a project with a shifting population of predominantly White, middle- and upper-middle-class graduate students, and me: a White, female university professor–researcher. Thus, the most salient issues that informed the relationships between and among the young people, me, and the other members of the university-based team were related to race, age, educational status, and social class.

I have a history of antiracist work and thus entered the Bridgeport project from a different position than the members of the university-based team, many of whom had never addressed racism in themselves or in their workplaces. That is not to suggest that I was not challenged by my own whiteness and racism during the course of the project. I was. Yet I have ·een addressing issues of whiteness and racism, both personally and ˙ofessionally, for many years. Thus, I had a set of strategies in place to sist me as I negotiated race-related issues within the research process.

The team members entered the project differently. They came to the research process with an accumulation of stereotypical beliefs about 3ridgeport. For example, Vonnie stated that "it is full of violence, drugs, and crime." Sarah, another member of the research team, stated that she had grown up "in an affluent White community that borders Bridgeport. I learned growing up that Bridgeport was a dangerous place and had some seedy sections that were to be avoided at all costs" (McIntyre, 2000, p. 30).

These kinds of stereotypes kept the members of the research team from developing relationships with the young people that were untainted by prejudice, fear, and uncertainty. Like Sarah, the majority of the team members grew up in well-resourced, mainly White communities and attended predominantly White educational institutions. Until they joined the PAR project, they had little experience addressing racism or working with young people of color. Thus, the team members often found themselves struggling with how to relate to the young people as co-collaborators in a research process.

The team members and I had multiple, sometimes heated discussions about whiteness, racism, and our experiences with both. Those discussions were highly significant in that they challenged the team members to rethink their prior beliefs about Bridgeport, about people of color, and about themselves as Whites. Rethinking their beliefs led the team members to rethink their actions. By changing their actions, they became more confident in themselves and in their abilities to be proactive in their positions as collaborators with the young people in the project.

The team members and I did not eliminate all the stereotypes and false beliefs that we brought to the PAR project. Yet by continually reflecting on our personal histories and by working to eliminate stereotypical beliefs about ourselves and others, the team members learned how to listen to the participants *so as to learn from them*—a valuable and important skill in participatory action research (see McIntyre, 2003).

Just as the members of the research team and I engaged in ongoing discussions about how we addressed our experiences with racism and whiteness, the young people also discussed the ways in which racism and whiteness structured *their* lives. Many times during the project, the participants discussed what it is like for them to be African American, Puerto Rican, and Dominican, to live in an urban community, and to attend an urban school. They told stories about being asked to leave stores in a wealthy town adjacent to Bridgeport because they were Black or Brown; how "Teachers won't come to our school 'cause there's drugs and weapons in the school, and they think all the kids are lazy and stupid" (Collin); and how some of them "sneak out of the house at night 'cause when you live in the projects, your mother never wants to let you out" (Blood).

In addition, the young people articulated their perspectives about what it was like to "hang out with White people" (Tee).

Melinda: There are some White people who are OK. Like you people from the university. You're OK White people. But then there are White people like the ones that came to help us with the cleanup project. They act like we don't know what we're doin'. Like they're the smart ones 'cause they're White.

Rebecca: Yeah, then there's other White people, ya know, the ones who think they got it goin' on. Like they just make me sick. Thinkin' they all that.

Tee: Yeah, and then there's the rest of the Whites who are always just dissin' us all the way around.

The young people's willingness to explore issues of race throughout the research process affirmed for me the possibilities that exist in PAR to create spaces for rich and critical dialogue between youth of color and "OK White people"—dialogue that contributed to the building of trusting and respectful relationships between the participants, me, and the rest of the university-based team.

In the Belfast project, the women and I shared gender, racial, and social class identities. Although I was the only one to hold a doctoral degree, some of the women were college graduates, and two of the women were enrolled in master's programs. Thus, though significant, issues of race, social class, age, and educational status did not cause friction between the women and me. Rather, they provided a sense of shared experience that helped us to forge relationships as women, friends, and researchers.

The women and I *did* grapple with other issues, though, as we engaged the PAR project. Sometimes my status as a researcher, a foreigner, an outsider, and someone who had not shared many of the life experiences that shaped the women's lives resulted in moments of disconnection between the women and me. During those times, the women focused on my role as an academic, as the one who "knew" what to do and how to do it (see Chapter Two). I repeatedly informed the women that they were the "real knowers" of their lives and that I had complete confidence in them and in their abilities to make decisions that reflected the goals they had for themselves and for the project. Many times, they responded to my compliments with humor and a few choice words about how they did not "know much about all that much" (Michelle). Yet as the project evolved and as the women concretized aspects of the project, they became more confident in claiming what they knew and in using their knowledge to make change. They, like the young people, transformed dialogue into action and contributed to developing a collaborative process of reflection and change that reflected their desires and fulfilled many of their research goals.

Ethical Challenges in Participatory Action Research

How participants and practitioners view their responsibilities within a PAR project is linked to a number of ethical questions that arise during collaborative processes of change. Given the particularities of PAR, the sites where projects take place, the people involved, the issues under investigation, and the unique features that characterize specific projects, it is impossible to address all of them here. Some, like issues of authority, access to resources, and defining the issue to be examined, are self-evident at the beginning of many PAR processes. Others, like relationship building, addressing research questions, and deciding who will participate, who will speak for whom, who "owns" the data generated in a PAR project, what actions will be taken, and how information will be disseminated to outsiders, usually materialize as the process evolves.

Those issues, as well as others, are not unique to participatory action research. Over many decades, a number of professional organizations across a number of disciplines have provided guidelines and codes of behavior that guide particular types of community-based research (Trimble & Fisher, 2005). Aspects of those guidelines framed the two PAR projects described herein. I present them as points of entry into thinking through some of the issues that may arise in participatory processes of reflection and action. They are not the only guidelines, nor may they be the most

salient ones for each PAR project. Yet they are the ones that provided me with a structure for framing principled and trustworthy research processes in Belfast and Bridgeport.
Ethical considerations in PAR:

1. Participants engage in *all* aspects of the project.
2. Practitioners have an appreciation of the capacity for individuals to work together to effect change.
3. Practitioners participate *with* participants in the overall PAR process, contributing resources and knowledge when necessary.
4. Attention is given to reducing barriers between participants and practitioners of participatory action research. That includes coconstruction of consent procedures, documentation of data, and ensuring that the language used in the research project is understood by participants.
5. Participants are encouraged to learn about research methods that are appropriate to the project.
6. Practitioners make a distinction between professional ethical considerations and contextually specific ethical considerations, which can be negotiated and modified to best serve the participants.
7. Practitioners take every precaution to protect the confidentiality, privacy, and identity of participants.
8. Practitioners do not disseminate any research data without the explicit consent of those involved.
9. Practitioners are trustworthy; scrupulous in their efforts to give primacy to participants' goals; responsible for the well-being of all involved; fair, just, and willing to relinquish their agendas if they conflict with participants' desires.

It is my belief that practitioners of PAR must take the first step in openly addressing the ethical challenges that occur in PAR projects. It is up to them to ensure that participants are not left in situations that compromise their safety and/or that leave them vulnerable and at risk. In addition, practitioners of PAR must do more than simply follow a set of ethical guidelines; they must *be* ethical, honest, and forthright people. If not, their presence will be seen by the group of people they hope to work with as an intrusion; as just another researcher engaged in a "drive-by" research project that benefits the researcher and leaves the participants with nothing.

It is also up to practitioners to give primacy to the participants' perspectives, realities, and truths within the research process. That is not to suggest that local actors' realities and narratives about those realities are less characterized by issues of power, authority, and community status. It *is* to suggest that many participants of PAR projects have not had the opportunity to speak their truths into public life and therefore must be provided with space to do so.

There is no *one* way to engage in PAR that alleviates the many ethical issues and inherent risks that are threaded throughout PAR projects. Nor does simply acknowledging those issues and risks in published accounts assuage the unintended consequences that accompany reflection/action-based projects. Rather, addressing power, authority, the interrelationship of race, gender, social class, level of education, and ability, as well as a host of issues noted in this book, requires a deep commitment by researchers and participants to work together to provide equity, safety, and parity in resources within the PAR process.

Wadsworth (1998) argues that PAR "involves an imaginative leap from a world of 'as it is' to a glimpse of the world 'as it could be'" (p. 6). In our quest to take that leap, it is incumbent upon practitioners of PAR to take seriously the realities of "what is" for local actors in PAR projects. In addition, we need to take seriously what "could be" in PAR projects and do so by maintaining an ethical and transparent stance that engenders trust and reciprocity with the people who invite us into their lives.

2

PARTICIPATION

What It Means and How It Works

McTaggart (1997b) highlights the distinction between "involvement" and "participation" in participatory action research. He states that authentic participation means that the participants share "in the way research is conceptualized, practiced, and brought to bear on the life-world" (p. 28). This is in contrast to being merely "involved" in PAR, where one does not have ownership over or in the project.

I agree with that distinction and further argue that what is important to and in a PAR project is the *quality* of the participation that people engage in, not the proportionality of that participation. It is my experience that the most effective strategy for engaging people in PAR projects is for the participants and the researchers to make use of "commonsense" participation. In other words, to take joint responsibility for developing *the group's* version of what it means to participate in a PAR process. When researchers and participants work together to define the most practical and doable ways for them to participate, there is less pressure on individuals to conform to *a* way of participating. In that way, participation is viewed as a choice, not an imposition.

In this chapter, I discuss the various ways in which the women in Belfast and the young people in Bridgeport participated in their respective projects. In so doing, I demonstrate how participation in processes of self- and collective reflection and action increases the likelihood that what groups learn in and through those processes can be put into practice in ways that benefit those involved.

DEFINING AND EXPERIENCING PARTICIPATION

No matter what issue is under investigation or what problem participants and researchers hope to address, it is important to be clear about the basic terms related to participatory action research. Therefore, in each project, and in language that was accessible to both groups, I explained the history and some of the basic principles of participatory action research. In the case of the young people, I invited them to discuss how *they* would define participatory action research.

The young people decided to look up the words *participation, action,* and *research* in the dictionary. After we discussed the definitions they found, I invited them to define those terms in ways that would be useful for them as we began the PAR process. The young people decided on the following definitions: "Participation means being part of the group and paying attention to what it is we're doing. Action means that we all have to agree to do things that are good for the project." Finally, the participants decided that research, a term they were familiar with owing to their experiences in science class, meant "investigating and studying things so you can understand them better" (November 24, 1997).

I congratulated the young people on developing definitions to frame the project and then offered two suggestions about how they might capitalize on "participation." I suggested that they be consistent in their attendance at group sessions and that they actively engage in project-related activities.

The participants agreed that it was important for them to be consistent in their attendance and to be active in the group sessions. Then they engaged in a long discussion about what would happen if they chose *not* to attend the sessions on a regular basis or *not* to participate in project-related activities. Tee stated that he didn't think people should be "kicked out of the project just because we don't participate once in a while." Risha agreed, stating that the participants should be given "more chances than just one to show that we really do want to belong to the project."

Since that was the general feeling among all the participants, they decided that for the project to work effectively, they needed to sign contracts. The contracts the participants created and signed stipulated that if someone came to the sessions and refused to participate more than three times, that person would be asked to leave the project. When I asked the participants what they meant by "refuse to participate," they said, "Like if they're foolin' around and you ask them to stop or everyone is tellin' them to stop and they just keep actin' the fool, that's when they're not participating" (Tina). The same consequence applied, they said, if someone missed three sessions "without a good excuse." If the person did not have a good excuse, which the participants defined as "being sick, having to stay after school, taking a test, or going to the dentist, something like that" (Collin), then they would be asked to leave the project.

When I asked the participants who was responsible for ensuring that people fulfilled their contracts, they said that everyone, including me and the other members of the university-based team, was responsible for making sure that people participated. If there were disagreements about a person's level of participation then the young people decided that everyone in the project would vote on whether the person should be asked to leave the project or be given another chance.

Ongoing discussions about individual and collective participation were threaded throughout the project. That is because the young people changed their minds, became distracted with life, and, on occasion, lost interest in the project. Sometimes that lost interest manifested itself in a participant's absence from a session. Other times, it manifested itself in the fact that certain participants shirked project-related responsibilities.

My response to the young people's negligence and/or forgetfulness during the project was to ask a simple question: "What type of project are we engaged in?" Their response was always the same, and always delivered in unison: "Participatory." Once the response was delivered, we reviewed the meaning of participation and discussed the most effective ways for the participants to complete project-related tasks. The secretary (a position the participants created as a way to keep track of what was discussed and decided upon in the group sessions) reviewed her or his notes and informed us who was responsible for what task. The group then discussed why certain activities were completed and others were not, and why some people accomplished their goals and others "failed to do their jobs, even though they signed a contract" (Veronica). If it was something the participants deemed out of their control—for example, if a person went to see a teacher about a project-related activity and the teacher was not there, or if a person was supposed to get the school's calendar but the school secretary said it was not available—then the young people took the view that the participant involved should not be blamed. As Monique stated, "They tried. That should count for something. That shouldn't be counted as one of the three times they didn't do what they said they'd do."

During the project, there were multiple times when the young people "didn't do what they said they'd do"—at least when they said they would do it. Nonetheless, they were able to accomplish many of their goals and do so without "kicking anyone out of the project."

The process of linking the *meaning* of participation to the *actualization* of participation was slow and time-consuming. There were times when we spent entire sessions solely discussing the meaning of "participation." Yet it was in those discussions that the young people realized that if they wanted things to happen, they were the ones who had to *make* them happen. They recognized that if they wanted to organize a school assembly, they had to do the work to make that happen. If they wanted to design a photo-text book, they had to take the necessary photographs and write the necessary texts. If they wanted to invite government officials, representatives of the media, and community members to their various events, they needed to contact them. If they wanted to present their work to faculties, students, funders, and other interested parties, they needed to craft presentations.

They also recognized that before they could improve things in their community that they found disturbing, they needed to become critically aware of what those things were. That awareness would only come when they participated in activities that generated knowledge, ideas, and plans of action. As Tee stated: "You have to be willing to participate and do what you said you'd do. If you do that, then you do somethin' good for the community." Tonesha agreed, then added, "Even if you don't like what you're doin' sometimes, if you said you're gonna do it, you gotta do it."

DIMENSIONS OF PARTICIPATION: WOMEN AND PARTICIPATORY ACTION RESEARCH

For the 2 years that the women and I engaged in the PAR project, we met in a conference room in the Reccy—the name local residents gave to the local recreation/community center. While we worked in the conference room, two teenage girls cared for the women's children in the all-purpose room down the hall.

With the knowledge that their children were close by and being cared for, the women were free to concentrate on the topics generated in the sessions. As important, they were free to be present to one another in an environment where the women could, as Nóra stated, gain "a sense of shared experiences in some way; a sense of support . . . a feelin' of havin' time just for us, d'ya know what I mean? Of havin' time set aside for yourself is lovely" (McIntyre, 2004, p. 28).

The women did experience "lovely" moments during the project. At the same time, they were challenged by participating in a process in which they felt they were "baring our souls for all to see" (Lucy). The women's hesitation to participate in a collective experience that would provide them with opportunities to reveal aspects of their lives to one another, to me, and to the outside community was due, in part, to the silence that characterizes their lives. This silence is and was a legitimate response to the war and its aftermath. Like many who grew up in the Troubles, the women were taught never to speak to the police or anyone in a uniform; not to answer any question put to them by someone they did not know; not to trust any adult who was not introduced to them by someone in the community; not to walk out of the community by themselves; and not to frequent particular stores, restaurants, movie theaters, and recreation areas. In the PAR project, the women were invited to explore those silences— an invitation that the women accepted but did not always act on. Inviting the women to speak about their lives and address issues that were and are painful to or unresolved for them presupposed that they could decline the invitation and be selective about what they revealed at any given moment during the research process (McIntyre, 2004). The women's silences—and the decisions they made to break those silences at different moments in the PAR project—reflect the degree to which they felt safe participating in group dialogue and later in the action steps they chose to enact.

In addition to the silence that informed the women's engagement in the project, a different kind of discomfort emerged when the women engaged in project-related activities—a discomfort born of self-consciousness. The women's self-consciousness was most evident when I invited them to participate in creative activities like drawing, sculpting, and painting. The minute the women saw the magic markers, the paint, or the clay, they pushed their chairs away from the table and told me that they "couldn't draw, couldn't write, and didn't know how to use clay to tell a story" (Winnie). When the women did not want to engage in a particular activity, they left the room for an extended cigarette break, repeatedly changed the topic under discussion, and/or asked other women in the group to do the activity for them.

I repeatedly encouraged the women to "give the activities a try" and view the activities as integrative, educative, and a natural method for self- and collective inquiry. The women usually laughed at my "cheerleading," telling me, "The real reason we'll pick up a paint brush, Alice, is 'cause you flew over here just for us and we're known for our hospitality" (Lucy).

Humor was a significant factor in the PAR project and lubricated the process in many important ways. It was the women's humor—directed at me and at themselves—that assisted us in accepting our insecurities and discomforts. In addition, when the women acknowledged their self-consciousness and accepted it as an important dynamic in the project, they were more willing to participate in the various activities, "even though," as Deirdre said, "we don't know what the hell we're doin'."

It is my experience working with the young people and the women that their resistance to various project-related activities was a normal response to processes of self- and collective exploration. Engaging in processes of reflection and revelation can be anxiety producing for people who are unaccustomed to speaking freely, expressing themselves through multiple modalities, and voicing their fears, hurts, hopes, and suggestions for change.

Yet in the case of the projects described here, the participants ultimately allowed themselves to be vulnerable in front of others. As a result of working through their discomfort and self-consciousness, the women and the young people came to see that their participation in their respective projects provided them with unique opportunities to express themselves to each other, to me, and to outside communities.

USING MULTIPLE MODALITIES TO GENERATE PARTICIPATION AND CONSTRUCT KNOWLEDGE

Reason (1993) posits that "Research based on self-study requires that we adopt an extended epistemology which moves between and seeks to integrate several different kinds of knowing" (p. 1259). How practitioners of PAR decide which "kinds of knowing" participants decide to utilize is dependent on the aim and the context of the project. For example, secondary sources like reports, statistics, files, and historical documents are invaluable tools for gathering important information that contributes to project-related data, and practitioners of PAR make use of those sources when needed.

As important are the primary sources that are utilized as tools for gathering and constructing knowledge within PAR projects. In communities worldwide, participants and practitioners of PAR employ long-standing indigenous methods of knowing so as to maintain and sustain communities' histories, traditions, and practices. Equally valuable is the integration of creative methods with local ways of knowing—methods that unearth, uncover, and sometimes undo "what we know" so as to "know anew." The effectiveness of these methods—for example, mapping, diagramming, role-playing, drama, music, art, and movement—is dependent, as described above, on the participants' willingness to engage in them, as well as the methods' applicability to the project.

Many of the above methods have been utilized for decades in a variety of academic disciplines—for example, anthropology, sociology, psychology, community development, feminist research, and popular theater (Mikkelsen, 2001). For instance, Cornwall and Jewkes (1995) used body mapping in a PAR project with Zimbabwean women so they could visualize the differences between Western and non-Western medical models. The visualizations assisted the women in gaining a better understanding of how to take care of their bodies. Lykes (2001) used dramatizations, masks, and movement with women and children in Guatemala, which provided the project's participants with opportunities to "enact the unspeakable stories of violence and destruction they had survived or witnessed" (p. 364) during their country's 30-year war. Rocheleau, Ross, Morrobel, and Hernandez (1998) used landscape mapping with the people of Zambrana-Chacuey in the Dominican Republic to explore the gender- and class-divided regions where the participants of their project lived and worked. Preston-Whyte & Dalrymple (1996) utilized a drama-based AIDS education program with young people in KwaZulu-Natal, South Africa, to increase awareness of AIDS. By engaging in traditional healing circles, Dickson was better able to understand the use of ceremonies and practices in determining how to develop health programs for Aboriginal grandmothers living in Canada (Dickson & Green, 2001).

Veroff (2002) used printmaking, video, and drawing to explore questions of identity, culture, and power with young Inuit adults in a PAR project in Montreal, Quebec. The interweaving of artistic creation and production provided the participants with opportunities "to be critical about what was happening to them and gave them the desire to take action for themselves" (p. 1286). Spaniol (2005) also used an arts-based approach with art therapists who were interested in using PAR with people suffering from various forms of mental illness.

In the above examples, and many others not included here, participants were introduced to experiential methods of constructing knowledge. Although the methods used were unfamiliar to many of the participants, their effectiveness was evident as the projects proceeded. One reason for their effectiveness is that visual, hands-on activities can equalize the relationships "between the literate and illiterate, between the marginalized and the self-confident" (Mikkelsen, 2001, p. 118). In addition, using multiple modalities in PAR projects contributes to a rich and nuanced body of knowledge that can be used to effect change.

In the Bridgeport project, the young people generated knowledge by creating group collages to represent "community"; taking neighborhood walks to gather information about their surroundings; developing a skit to perform at a school assembly; designing logos for T-shirts, banners, and newsletters; and engaging in various forms of storytelling and symbolic art. In Belfast, the women also created collages that represented their community. In addition, they created stories with clay, designed symbols reflecting the experiences of Irish women, and painted images based on Maya Angelou's poem "Still I Rise" (Angelou, 1994).

In each site, the use of nontraditional strategies for tapping into the participants' experiences, thoughts, ideas, and emotions provided individuals with unique ways to express themselves. In both projects, there was no standard, predetermined criteria for what constituted a "great" collage, a "perfect" drawing, or an "extraordinary" image. Rather, each participant began with a blank slate. Sometimes, as noted above, that blank slate evoked feelings of self-consciousness and resistance. Other times, it evoked a sense of possibility and excitement. Either way, it assisted all of us in generating a host of "knowledges" in thought-provoking and imaginative ways.

THE CHALLENGES AND POSSIBILITIES OF USING PHOTOVOICE IN PAR

One creative-based method for generating knowledge that both participant groups engaged in was photovoice—an approach to investigating phenomena in which people utilize photography to raise awareness and make change (see, e.g, Wang, 1999; Ewald, 2001; Wu et al., 1995; Women of ADMI & Lykes, 2000; and McIntyre, 2000, 2004). The photovoice projects we implemented in Bridgeport and Belfast enabled the women and the young people to document aspects of their communities, and of their daily lives, from their own perspectives. Once documented, the two groups crafted text to accompany their photographs, thus providing outsiders with insiders' knowledge about aspects of their communities that they take great pride in, and, as important, have great concerns about.

A number of questions framed the participants' photovoice projects—questions that, like PAR, are not "fixed." Rather, they were entry points into yet more questions, more opportunities for reflecting on how to most effectively develop a photovoice project, and more ideas about how to address the issues under investigation through photography. (For a list of sample questions see Figure 2.1.)

To initiate the photovoice project in Bridgeport, each participant was given a camera and two rolls of film. They were given 5 days to take photographs of their community (see McIntyre, 2000, for a more detailed account of the photovoice project). The photographs the young people took revealed powerful images of their daily lives. Some of their photographs were provocative, others humorous, and still others disturbing. I was particularly struck by Blood's photographs, particularly one he took of a seagull flying over the housing project where he lives. As I reviewed Blood's photographs with him, I informed him that he had quite a knack for photography.

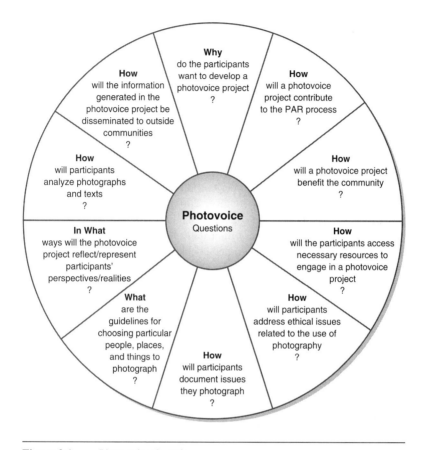

Figure 2.1   Photovoice Questions

About an hour after I spoke to Blood, he walked up behind me, slipped something into my hand, and walked away. I looked down and saw the photograph of the seagull—which now has a prominent place in my office. That was the first time during the initial 8 months of the project that Blood initiated any type of interaction with me. Although he participated in the activities, Blood rarely spoke to me or to his peers during the group sessions. It was not until we implemented the photovoice project that Blood became an active participant in the project and engaged in the group's decision-making processes.

Blood's participation in the research process was not unique. To some degree, all of the young people were challenged by the various dimensions of what it means to participate in a PAR project. What was unique about Blood's participation is that it was so closely linked to the use of photography as a method of self-expression and knowledge generation. Using the camera was a catalyst for many of the participants in terms of concretizing particular aspects of the project. For Blood, the camera also represented a vehicle for self-expression that he did not experience in school, a setting that emphasizes verbal skills for demonstrating knowledge and mastery of one's skills (McIntyre, 2000).

The women in Belfast also experienced a range of emotions as a result of engaging in photovoice. In October 2000, I provided the women with two Instamatic cameras—one color and one black-and-white—and invited them to tell a visual story about their daily lives. To photograph multiple aspects of the community, the women decided to document their lives over a 9-month period. I visited the women three times during that period to collaborate with them in their picture-taking.

Kay, one of the women who participated in the project, was, like Blood, a quiet participant in group discussions and project-related activities. Kay willingly engaged in collage-making, painting, and taking photographs for the photo-text exhibit the women designed. Yet as the sessions evolved and as the women revealed more about their lives and the ways in which the war shaped their understandings of themselves and their community, Kay withdrew. She arrived late to a session one day; left early another day. One weekend we had scheduled two day-long sessions, and Kay missed both of them. The women informed me that she was "still around" but that she was having a few problems in her life and found it difficult to attend the group sessions.

During one of my visits to Belfast, I visited Kay and, over a cup of tea, filled her in on what we were doing in the group meetings. Kay apologized for missing the sessions but told me that she needed to spend that time with her children. Kay went on to tell me that she suffers from depression and that "sometimes I have a hard time talking in groups, Alice, and that is no reflection on the group. . . . It's just that sometimes I get very down and feel like I'm not really part of what's going on around me" (McIntyre, 2004, p. 61).

Kay informed me that she enjoyed the project, that she was still taking photographs, but that "It's too much for me to participate in the sessions, look at everyone's photographs, mine, too, and think about the stories that everyone is telling about them." I assured Kay that I understood and that although she was not present at the sessions, the women and I wanted her to know that she remained a participant in the project.

Kay did not return to the group sessions on a consistent basis. The unveiling of the silences, the consciousness-raising discussions, the symbolic art that evoked the women's experiences with the war, the storytelling, and the overall self- and collective inquiry and scrutiny that marked the women's discussions were, as Kay said, "too much" for her. Unlike Blood, who was a quiet participant for months until he found a vehicle for expressing himself, Kay found self-expression too anxiety producing. Therefore, Kay's participation took the form of a cup of tea in her home, a drink at the local pub, or a chat on the corner of Monument Road.

How Kay participated in the project made little difference to me or to the other women. When we spoke about the participants of the project, we included Kay. When we told outsiders who was responsible for that painting or that image, we included Kay. She may not have participated as fully as the others, or as consistently, but she did participate in a way that genuinely spoke to her desire to stay connected to the women and that contributed to the overall story of what life is like for women in the Monument Road community.

Blood's experience as a participant in the Bridgeport project, and Kay's in the Belfast project, are key to understanding the importance of researchers and participants negotiating the parameters of participation, particularly in communities characterized by conflict. The participation of people living in conflicted communities in the context of a PAR project is always in flux, always fluid, and always unpredictable. In the Bridgeport and Belfast projects, participants had personal or familial illnesses, work responsibilities, out-of-town commitments, after-school programs, school transfers, and a host of other things that made it impossible for them to be present at certain moments in the project.

Their absence, and the absence of any participant in an ongoing PAR project, briefly or for the long term, raises questions about how participants reach consensus, build community, and share responsibilities. In addition, it raises important questions about how a missing participant's information is integrated into the interpretations of the research data. Given the context-specific nature of PAR, those questions are not easily answered. Yet in whatever context a PAR project is played out, it is my experience that practitioners and participants must remain flexible, open to redefining the meaning of "participation" as the process evolves, and willing to integrate the unexpected if they want to maintain and sustain the research process.

NEGOTIATING THE ROLE OF
PRACTITIONER AND PARTICIPANT

As a practitioner of PAR, one of my responsibilities is to enhance partici-pation and capitalize on participants' skills and capabilities. As I do so, I need to remember that *the participants* are the key decision makers, the ones responsible for how, when, and why a project proceeds. That did not mean that I was not a participant in the decision-making processes as they evolved in the Belfast and Bridgeport projects. I was. Yet it was my respon-sibility to embody that role in ways that reflected *the participants'* desires to move their projects in particular directions.

For that to occur in Bridgeport, I needed to continually remind the young people that I was not their teacher. I was not there to "make them do this" or "force them to do that." I was a practitioner, a participant, a resource, but I was *not* the teacher, the leader, or the sole authority who determined the actions that would be taken within the context of the project.

That was a challenging notion for the young people to grasp. They had been in school for 6 years when I met them. Thus, they were familiar with the all-too-common paradigm in the educational system in the United States—the transmission of knowledge from the teacher to the student (Freire, 1970). They had not been encouraged to question authority, chal-lenge established knowledge, or participate in their own learning. Thus, the young people were unsure of how to respond when I invited them to par-ticipate in a learning process in which they were the principal players.

As the young people learned how to take responsibility for various aspects of the project, I learned how to step away from "taking over" aspects of the project that I felt strongly about. For example, one of the things the young people wanted to do in the PAR project was to create a photo-text book that they wanted to publish and disseminate to the commu-nity. I presented the participants' ideas about a photo-text book to a friend of mine who is a graphic designer. During a group session, I informed the participants that my friend agreed to assist us in creating such a book. I told them that she offered to show us how to scan photographs, create montages of images, and situate text to reflect the meanings of the photographs that would be highlighted in the book. The participants thought that my friend's ideas were "cool" and that designing a book would be "really fun to do."

I wanted to capitalize on my friend's availability and felt that if everyone participated on a consistent basis, while also taking responsibility for other project-related activities, we could make some headway in designing the book. It was that "want" that prompted me to remind the participants, on a regular basis, that, in conjunction with their other responsibilities, they might want to carve out time for us to formulate a plan regarding the photo-text book.

Although the participants were excited about designing a book, they did not particularly want to craft it on *my* timetable. As Tonesha clearly stated during one of the sessions, "We don't have enough time to work on every-thing, Dr. McIntyre. We have the assembly, the presentations, going to city hall, and learning a dance for our skit. So, let's put the book away until we finish the other projects. Everyone who agrees, raise your hand." Immediately, all the participants raised their hands. It was not until 6 months later that we began working on the photo-text book, and it was a full year and a half before the project was completed (see One STEP Group, McIntyre, & McKeirnan, 2000).

The above example, and others I experienced in both projects, reveals the importance of practitioners' "getting out of the way" and allowing people to proceed in ways that make sense to and for them—not necessarily to and for the practitioner. That does not mean that participants do not need an occasional push or a gentle prodding now and then. It is my experience with the women and the young people that they did, and they oftentimes looked to me to do that. I was a coparticipant in the projects and, like them, brought a particular set of skills, knowledge, and resources to the groups that needed to be used in practical ways so as to contribute to the overall research process.

"YOU'RE GONNA BE THE TELLER, BUT IT'S OURS"

In the Belfast project, there were times when the women were unsure of their decision-making abilities and turned to me for support, guidance, and assis-tance. I was more than willing to provide all of the above, yet I also reminded the women that they were capable of making decisions on their own. Sometimes the women responded to my comments with humor and sarcasm. Other times, the women clearly expected me to "fix" the problem at hand.

Below, I present an excerpt from a discussion that was generated after the women attempted to analyze photographs for the photo-text project they were creating. I began the discussion by asking the women if they had collectively agreed on the categories they wanted to use to interpret their photographs.

Lucy: So is this [the photos and the categories they chose] all right, Alice? Or do you want more? Geez, you'll be drawin' blood in a minute.

Alice: It's not that I want more. I just, it's up to you. I mean, you either agree on some photos or you don't agree on others, and it seems like you don't all agree here. Which is fine as long as that is taken into account when you interpret the meanings of the photographs.

Lucy: What d'ya mean? . . . Are ya sayin' we just stuck them there? . . . Is that what you're sayin'?

Tricia: Yeah, she is.

Lucy: You're pickin' on us.

Alice: From my perspective, to leave here and say to people outside the community, "OK, this is what this group said" when it hasn't been thought through and reflected upon, I think does you a disservice. So, it might feel like I'm picking on you, but from my point of view, I don't want to misrepresent the work that you've done.

(crosstalk)

Winnie: We want to represent ourselves right as well, and that's why we're relyin' on you more in this part of the project . . . because ya know, that's really personal to us, but are we representin' ourselves and our community well? And articulatin' it? Because it's very hard to describe yourself sometimes. You sort of have to get justification from someone. D'ya know what I mean? I'm askin' you.

(crosstalk)

Lucy: But I'm not, I'm not sayin' that I want you to tell me or to tell us what to do. What I'm sayin' is we have never done this before. You have done it before workin' with the kids in Bridgeport and puttin' a book and stuff together. We've never done this before. So what I'm sayin' is, ya need to be more clear, to guide us, for us to understand.

Winnie: But I know, Alice, you don't want to do that too much either because you don't want to put your mark on it 'cause it's our community; it's not your community.

Deirdre: I feel as well that somehow we put you in a position because you're Alice, and you're our friend now. And that's the way we want it to be, so we're chattin' away and tellin' you all these things and talkin' to you and whatever, and then we just switch and go like that, "Well, you're the professor. You must know . . . You tell us. What do we know? We live on [Monument] Road, ya know? We're the white mice. You tell us." And I know that's not very fair, and I imagine you must feel it in the position you're in because you have those two roles to fill, but we turn them on and off when we want . . . So, yeah, it's a different dynamic this time around, but at the same time, we want kinda guidance. Maybe we're not very nice about askin' for it. We don't do it very well . . . 'Cause it is our story to tell, not yours, if you know what I mean. You're gonna be the teller, but it's ours. (McIntyre, 2004, p. 99–100)

After this exchange we had lengthy conversations about my roles and responsibilities as a practitioner and a friend. I agreed with the women that I had experience as a researcher and as someone who had analyzed and interpreted data. I also agreed with the women when they asserted that they were the primary tellers of their stories. I informed them that the challenge *for me* was deciding to what extent I needed to assist them in that story-telling process.

As evidenced by the women's discussion, they felt strongly that I needed to assist them in analyzing the stories and discussions that were linked to their photographs. Therefore, during the next session, I demonstrated a number of analytical strategies to assist the women in making meaning of their photographs. Some of the strategies the women decided to use were helpful; others confused them. In the end, the women decided on an analytical strategy that worked for *them*—a strategy that was a combination of other researchers' work and their own ideas for making sense of their visual stories. (See McIntyre, 2004, for a more detailed account of how the women engaged the analysis process.)

As noted earlier, it is my experience that the most effective strategy for engaging people in a PAR project is for the participants and the researchers to use commonsense participation and to take joint responsibility for developing *the group's* version of what it means to participate in a PAR process. If both parties do not contribute to how people participate and in what ways, then practitioners of PAR run the risk of "telling" people how to do things, thus becoming too pedagogic and/or manipulative. Thus, they, and the participants, lose sight of the collaborative nature of the participant/ researcher relationship—a relationship that is vital to the effectiveness of a PAR project.

WHO BENEFITS? THE IMPORTANCE OF MULTIPLE PERSPECTIVES IN A PAR PROJECT

It is important to note that PAR projects are not initiated or carried out solely for the benefit of those who actually participate in the research process. The young people in Bridgeport demonstrated that although the majority of community residents did not participate in their cleanup project, the project itself benefited *all* members of the community. Similarly, the photovoice project that the women in Belfast designed and presented to outside audiences benefited their entire community because it represented images and stories that are usually ignored, dismissed, and overlooked in the overall story about how the residents of the Monument Road community experience their lives.

The reality is that many people living in communities where PAR projects take place do not participate in the actual research process. Some people are unable to commit themselves to a PAR project owing to work, family, and other responsibilities. Others choose not to participate owing to opposition to the idea of a project or to the direction they think the project might take. Still other people are unaware that a project is under way and may hear about it only as the project unfolds. Yet regardless of the reasons that people do not participate in a PAR project, the focus of the project should be to provide opportunities for local people to develop strategies and garner resources for changing their environments for the better. Thus, as many people as possible should be invited to participate, to voice their concerns, and to inquire as to the development of the PAR process as it evolves. As Kemmis and McTaggart (2005) suggest, "Not all will accept the invitation, but it is incumbent on those who do participate to take into account [those] others' understandings, perspectives, and interests" (p. 579).

PAR ACROSS CONTINENTS

Negotiating the role of practitioner and participant when I lived on one continent and the women in Belfast lived on another brought its own set of challenges to the PAR project. The fact that I live in the United States significantly informed the women's participation in the PAR project and predicated who would be responsible for project-related tasks. The women secured the conference room and found child-care providers. They also took the photographs that framed the photovoice project. I supplied materials for the project: cameras, film, tape recorders, audiotapes, food for the group meetings, and any last-minute items we needed upon my arrival in Belfast. In addition, I provided the funding for the project from sources in the United States. For the most part, the women and I were able to coordinate the PAR project without too much disruption to the project itself. Yet it is important to remember that daily life and unexpected events "get in the way" of participants' fulfilling project-related obligations. It is one thing for people to talk through an issue and make plans to take action on that issue during a group session; it is quite another for participants to walk out the door and fulfill project-related activities in the midst of their daily lives. That is one reason that the women readily admitted that maintaining the project at a pace that would move it forward was contingent upon *my* availability. Tricia summed up the feelings of the group one day when she said, "Without you, Alice, we forget. We get caught up in our lives. Plus, if we do all the work without you here, you won't come back."

Whether it is across continents or across town, practitioners need to employ the best methods available to facilitate processes in which participants can participate with one another to make change. That may mean that the projects do not always move at the pace the practitioner would like or in ways that satisfy everyone. Nonetheless, if the participation is authentic and if practitioners put their trust in people's desire to change, they affirm that participation is not an illusion but a material fact that provides energy, direction, and a sense of accomplishment to those involved.

CONCLUDING REFLECTIONS

Although the "ideal" PAR project may include participants who participate in *every* aspect of the project, it is my experience that, in reality, there are multiple factors that come into play when researchers and participants meet and decide to accompany one another through a collaborative process. It is unlikely that each party, individually or collectively, can or will participate equally in a PAR process. Nonetheless, the process by which individuals participate in PAR holds the most promise and the most potential in a participatory process. It is there, in that dialectical process of investigation and consciousness-raising, that participants rethink positions, imagine new ways of being, acting, and doing, and grapple with the catalytic energy that infuses PAR projects. It is by participating in critical dialogue, in discussions in which people agree, disagree, argue, debate, are affirmed for their views, and challenged for their views that participants truly experience the "aha" moments that come with self- and collective scrutiny. It is that type of participation that provides space for people to reflect on what is being discussed in the group sessions and then, upon reflection, to take the necessary steps to improve their current situations.

3

ACTION AND CHANGE IN PARTICIPATORY ACTION RESEARCH

The definition of action, in terms of how it is expressed in both scope and focus, is essentially limitless. Any concerted effort to remove some impediment that hampers the growth of a group of people, be it structural or ideological, could be defined as action within the framework of PAR.

(Kidd & Kral, 2005, p. 189)

In this chapter, I describe how the young people in Bridgeport and the women in Belfast participated in processes of critical reflection and dialogue that led to individual and collective action. First, I describe the process by which the young people developed a project aimed at cleaning up the Blair School community. The young people's decision to focus on the environment as an issue that needed the community's attention came about through months of dialogue in which we questioned existing knowledge, constructed new knowledge, interpreted collected data, and addressed the young people's desire to make positive changes in themselves and in their environment.

Second, I reveal the strategies the women in Belfast used to move from dialoguing about the realities of living in the Monument Road community to taking action to present those realities to outside communities. The women did not always experience those realities in similar ways. Yet they all believed that how they individually and collectively experienced a 35-year war needed to be told by those who lived through it and who continue to experience its aftermath.

"WE'RE IMPORTANT PEOPLE IN OUR COMMUNITY WHO MAKE A DIFFERENCE"

Like many adolescents, the young people experienced shifting attentions, moods, and interests as the project evolved, all of which influenced the decision-making process. In addition, there were shifting alliances within the group that oftentimes informed how and why the participants made certain decisions. When the young people were enthusiastic about a particular action they decided to take, they tended to disagree with one another and with me less often, argue about how to implement a certain action with less intensity, and refrain from pushing their own individual agendas.

For example, I asked the young people if they wanted to present aspects of their project to some faculty members and students at Boston College—an institution where a number of my colleagues were interested in the young people's work. I informed the participants that we could rent a van, drive to Boston, present our project, go out for pizza, and then have a "slumber party" at one of my relative's homes. The young people agreed that going to Boston was a great idea and immediately began to take action to accomplish that goal. We discussed the items that would be needed for us to organize the event. The young people needed to draft permission slips and letters explaining the trip to caregivers and parents, develop a presentation based on the work we were engaged in, choose photographs to reflect particular issues we wanted to focus on in the presentation, and craft a budget so we would have a general idea of how much funding we needed for the trip.

Over the course of the next few meetings, the young people accomplished all of the above: They crafted a letter to their parents and caregivers, drafted their presentation, chose appropriate photographs to accompany a presentation they cowrote with the university-based team, and generated a budget. They did so with little resistance and a good deal of excitement.

Not all the actions the young people took were accompanied by the collective enthusiasm the trip to Boston generated. For example, during the second year of the project, the participants realized that they had done "plenty of talkin' about how trashy our community is. Now, we gotta do somethin' about it" (Collin).

The "somethin'" they decided to do was develop a plan to clean up parts of their community. Some of the young people were hesitant to act on that idea because they believed it was "a waste of time" (Blood). Others believed that it was their responsibility to contribute to the upkeep of a community that suffers from neglect and lack of resources.

In the following excerpt, I illustrate one of the many discussions we engaged in regarding how the participants would address the environment. Although the young people lacked enthusiasm for cleaning up the community when the topic was initially discussed, their continued dialogue ignited new ideas, new ways of thinking and doing, and overall contributed to the development of a participant-initiated action plan.

Tee: We could make a cleanup group.

Monique: We did that once. Remember we cleaned all around the school?

Collin: Yeah, but this would be different. Not cleanin' just the school but cleanin' up the community.

Tee: I remember that day we cleaned up the school and we put a big sign in the front of the school. We could do that again. Only we could put up signs everywhere, like "Don't Put Garbage on the Ground," "Stop Littering," "Don't Make a Mess."

Blood: Where we gonna get the stuff?

Tonesha: Maybe we could get the school to give us some stuff. Or maybe ask people in the community to donate rakes and brooms. We have some money, Dr. Mac, right? We could buy garbage bags and those gloves that the garbage men wear.

Janine: But then what? It's gonna get dirty again.

Blood: Yeah, so let's just don't do it.

Alice: Well, you could not do it, or you could think of ways to do it and include other people in the community.

Collin: I said this last week, and I mean it. I think we need to be settin' an example for kids. This is our world, and we need to start cleanin' up our community now . . . Maybe the city will help us out a little bit, but only if we start puttin' effort into it.

Veronica: I did that school cleanup thing, too. But this would be different 'cause we'd be runnin' it—not the teachers. And we can get our friends to do it with us and the people in our neighborhood and some of the university people, and we could really clean the place up. 'Cause it sure needs it!

Puffy: I agree with y'all, but if I were y'all I wouldn't do it. People just go messin' it up again.

Alice: What would you do, Puffy?

William: I'm with Puffy. I'm not gonna keep on cleanin' places and then have people go make 'em dirty again.

Collin: You could at least try!

Puffy: Try and do what? Clean, then clean again, then keep on cleanin'?

Blood: What about we try it once? If people keep on dirtyin' it up, then we just don't do it anymore.

Mase: We could show them pictures. We could take pictures of dirty places, like the basketball court and the field and the houses on Main Street with all the junk in front of them.

(crosstalk)

Alice: Some of you are raising an important question, and that is: What if you take pictures, and inform the community, and ask the school to help you out, and use some of the grant money to buy things for the project, and a week later, the places you clean are dirty again?

Tonesha: So what? So it's dirty again? At least we did somethin'. And I think if we get people to help us, they'll help us keep it clean. Ya know how the school has those orange things they have us wear if we're crossing guards? We should have those for cleaning guards.

(laughter)

Monique: Yeah, we could walk all over the community with those on and make people pick up their trash. If they say, "No," we can pretend we're cops and give them tickets. (March 4, 1998)

For the next few weeks, the young people continued their discussions about forming a cleanup group. Many of the discussions they engaged in resembled the excerpt presented above: lots of give-and-take intertwined with disagreements, frustrations, humor, resistance, and the hope that they would find a solution to the issues that were of concern to them.

Out of those discussions, the participants ultimately agreed to "give the cleanup project a try" (Melinda). As part of the overall project, the participants decided to organize a schoolwide assembly, conduct a number of schoolwide activities, and present various aspects of the project to the Bridgeport city council and other community groups. There were numerous items the young people needed to act on each week to accomplish those goals. Some weeks, the participants broke into small groups, and each group took responsibility for a specific task. Other weeks, everyone collaborated on one particular issue.

One of the things the young people decided to do was design a symbol for their cleanup project that could be used on T-shirts, letterhead, and banners. I imagined that it would take a few short sessions to design such a symbol. I was wrong. It took almost 2 months for the young people to create a symbol. During that time, they argued about what size the symbol should be, what the symbol should represent, what color it should be, and how it should be positioned on T-shirts and letterhead.

For me, accompanying the young people as they came to a consensus about the symbol was a frustrating process. For them, it was a tug-of-war— a battle to see who was the best designer, the most creative artist, and the least likely to "come up with something stupid lookin'" (Blood). Whereas many of the sessions the participants engaged in were give-and-take dialogues that led to a particular action being taken, the process of designing a symbol for the group was characterized by a resistance to compromise and cooperation and a determination by a number of the young people to stand their ground when it came to how the group should represent itself.

Below, I present an excerpt from one of those group sessions. It reveals the challenges inherent in the young people's action-producing processes when their interests, attitudes, attention, and level of investment were in flux. It also reveals how PAR provided them with enough space to withstand the bumps and bruises that characterize humanizing experiences of reflection, action, and change.

Monique: I think we should make the school the symbol. Just draw the outside of the school and have that be it.

Mase: That's stupid. This isn't a school thing only. It's the community, too.

Tonesha: She isn't stupid just 'cause she has an idea. I think she's right. We could have the school in the symbol, and then if we want the community in it, we can think of something to do for that, too.

Janine: Like what?

Tonesha: I don't know. That's what we're doin' here, tryin' to figure it out.

Blood: I don't care what y'all do. Just do somethin'. I wanna go play ball.

Mase: Me, too.

Monique: Then why don't you go? We don't need you here anyway.

Tonesha: Yeah, we do. Mase, you can draw. Draw somethin' that we can use.

Melinda: Before we make a symbol, why don't we come up with a name for the project?

Risha: Yeah, that's a good idea.

Tee: How about "The Clean Machine"?

(laughter)

Mase: The Clean Machine. That's dumb.

Tee: Shut up. What idea do you have?

Blood: You shut up. Don't be tellin' someone else to shut up 'cause they don't like your idea.

Tonesha: Mind your business, Blood. Why don't you go play ball?

Melinda: It is his business. It's everyone's business.

Monique: No, it's not. It's only the business of people who want to say somethin' that helps the project.

Mase: Then say somethin'.

Monique: Why don't you—

Alice: Why don't we take a breath and try to focus on what you want to do here? We have spent a couple of months talking about the group, what we want to do, how we want to do it, and what resources we need to do some of the things you mentioned. We did all that with some arguments and disagreements, but overall, we accomplished a lot. Now we come to naming the project and coming up with a symbol, and we are stuck. Not to mention that you are being disrespectful to each other, something we've addressed before. So, can we start this session again and try to do two things. One, decide on a name, and two, decide on a symbol. Or we can take another route. How would you like to use the time we have today?

Blood: How about we just do the name for now?

Mase: Why? So you can play ball?

Melinda: See? It's always the boys. Can't just be quiet and do what needs to be done.

Tee: Just the boys? What about all them fights you girls have about the assembly and the skit you want to do?

Monique: But at least we do what we're supposed to do while we're fightin'. You all just keep interruptin' us, and we never get anythin' done.

Jason: Who's interruptin' now? Girls.

Monique: You shouldn't even talk after what you and Blood did in the cafeteria. Fightin' like a couple of dogs and makin' us miss the whole session.

Alice: OK, time for another deep breath. How about we begin with everyone thinking about a name they would like to call the group? We'll write the names on the chart paper and go from there. Unless you have another idea about how to formulate a name?

Risha: Good idea, Dr. Mac. If someone doesn't like her idea, go play ball because we made those rules way back, and if you don't want to participate, you have to leave 'cause you're botherin' everyone else. (October 13, 1999)

The above discussion ended without the young people taking any concrete action to name the group or design a symbol. That is not to suggest that the young people's conflicted dialogue was without merit. Although it may not have been productive at the time it occurred, the participants' disagreements ultimately prompted them to rethink how they were engaging in the project.

During the next group session, I invited the young people to listen to a portion of the audiotape from the above meeting. While listening, the participants laughed, appeared embarrassed, and, overall, realized how much time they wasted arguing with one another. I turned the tape recorder off and asked them if they wanted to try again to name their group and discuss what the symbol of the group might be. In unison, the participants stated that they wanted to give it another try, and, as Tee stated, "This time, we'll do it right."

What assisted the young people in moving forward with the project was that they became bored with their own apathy and with the petty arguments they engaged in. In addition, they knew that if they did not take control of the project and take the kinds of action they needed to take, the project would end. They were clearly aware that I and the other members of the university-based team were there to collaborate with them, participate in the activities they agreed on, act as resources when necessary, and basically accompany them in the project. They also realized that if they chose to sit back and do nothing, we would accept their decision to do that and step away from the cleanup project altogether. When faced with that decision—something that happened sporadically throughout the project—the young people recommitted themselves to developing strategies for moving the project forward.

The participants reviewed the goals they had already generated: to clean up portions of the community, involve the school and other people throughout the community in the project, write letters to government officials inviting them to join them in their efforts, take photographs to display at various venues so people could see the poor state of the community, and inform people beyond their particular community about how they, too, could clean up their neighborhoods and schools.

After we discussed the above goals, the young people brainstormed a host of names for the cleanup group—for example, "No More Talkin' Trash"; "Stop Messin' Around"; and "Take the First Step: Don't Litter." We wrote the names on chart paper and discussed the possibilities of the names mentioned. Those discussions led Tee to state that

> It's not just about us, though. It's about the earth. Like those Earth Days they have every year and we pay attention to the earth for that day. Well, we should pay attention to the earth every day. We can take the first step, like it says up there, and help clean up the earth.

Tee's observation led the young people to name their group, One STEP—the Save The Earth Program. Then they agreed that a symbol for the group would be a small hand-drawn picture of the earth with the words "Save the Earth Program" surrounding it.

It might appear that the act of coming up with a name for a group and designing a symbol for that group is a trivial exercise compared to the other issues the young people address in their everyday lives (e.g., education, community violence, and the negative effects of living in an underresourced urban community). Yet acting on something that people have control over is exactly the kind of thing that contributes to people's beliefs that they are creative, knowledgeable, and capable of making a difference in their own lives. Participatory action research offers people that opportunity—the opportunity to act on events that directly affect them and that contribute to their individual and collective well-being.

In the above example, the young people ultimately took control of the project and through collective effort and determination succeeded in organizing and implementing a cleanup event that brought attention to an issue that was salient to them. The participants were not able to enact the kind of widespread social change they hoped to generate in the project because it was not within their power to do so. Yet what they were able to do was exercise their power in realistic ways, in ways that were important to them, to their particular situation, and to the goals they had formulated for the overall PAR project.

"THAT'S US—FOR ALL THE WORLD TO SEE."

For many months, the women in Belfast and I discussed what action they would take to assist them in fulfilling their sometimes wavering desire to reveal their experiences living in and through a war to outside audiences. Unlike the young people's decision to take action regarding one issue— cleaning up the community—the women were focused on several issues. They wanted to present a version of their experiences as women growing up in and surviving a war that spoke to the multidimensionality of their individual lives, as well as to their collective commitment to maintaining and sustaining a community of well-being.

Arriving at the place where the women felt comfortable revealing their experiences to outsiders was a process intertwined with issues of power, authority, and identity. As with the young people, there were times when the women made decisions to act, or not to act, on a particular issue without conflict. For example, during one of the group sessions, I invited the women to use clay as a way to tell stories about their lives. I asked them to silently picture themselves sitting against a tree. On the other side of the tree was a storyteller. The storyteller was there to tell each of the women a story that she wanted to hear. I told the women it could be a historical story, a mystery, a fantasy, and/or a story about any person, place, or thing that came to mind. The women sat silently for about 5 minutes imagining the story they wanted the storyteller to relate to them. After that time of reflection, I invited each of the women to use modeling clay and create a symbolic representation of the story she had "heard."

The stories the women chose to represent with the clay focused on fairy tales, Irish history and folklore, and the relationship between the women's dreams and their everyday realities. The stories also addressed death, marriage, love, hope, and loss (McIntyre, 2004).

Deirdre's story focused on the death of a loved one. Winnie and Jacqueline wanted to understand the history behind old Irish folk tales they grew up listening to in their homes. Sorcha wanted to learn about the history of her family, and Tricia wanted to hear a story about what it would be like to meet a handsome prince and live her life "as if it was a fairy tale."

I thought the women's clay representations were creative and imaginative and vividly expressed the stories they generated. During a follow-up session, I asked the women if they would like to include their clay representations in the photo-text exhibit we were preparing for the West Belfast Festival. They immediately declined the invitation. I encouraged them to reconsider, telling them how I thought we could integrate their representations into the overall "story" the women were telling with their photographs and texts. I informed them that I thought there was a sense of hope threaded throughout their stories and that the narratives were significant links to other themes that had been generated in the project. According to Tricia, my encouraging comments were "falling on deaf ears."

Lucy:	Absolutely not, Alice. My clay figures look like my wee son did them.
Nóra:	I agree with Lucy. Bad enough we have to show people our photographs. I couldn't bear for them to see my attempt at using clay.
Sorcha:	Mine's crap. Nice colors, but I think we should roll the clay up and give it to the children.
Deirdre:	Are ya kiddin' with us, Alice? Ya must be kiddin' with us.
Jacqueline:	I could never let people see this.
Winnie:	That's your answer, Alice. No clay in the exhibit.

The women clearly made their views known. No action would be taken in terms of the clay stories. I, in turn, respected the women's decision, and thus we focused the exhibit solely on their photographs and texts.

That is not to say that the storytelling activity was not beneficial to the women and to the overall PAR process. The act of representing stories with clay was an important thread in the overall project and contributed to the themes the women generated as they developed the photo-text exhibit.

"WE FEEL GOOD ABOUT WHAT WE'RE DOIN' NOW IN THE PROJECT"

Despite the women's unanimous decision to *not* use the clay stories in their exhibit, there were mixed feelings among the women about how to present their photographs and texts to outside communities. For example, I showed the women images of the photo-text exhibit the young people in Bridgeport had created and showed them a photo-text book they had created as well. Some of the women liked the idea of producing a photo-text book more than they liked the idea of presenting their work via a photo-text exhibit. These women felt that a book "wouldn't embarrass us too much." Other women in the group disagreed, believing that a photo-text exhibit was more powerful and would provide viewers with an immediate connection to the women's lives.

The excerpt below represents one of the many discussions the women engaged in as they moved toward making a decision about how to act on the knowledge they generated in the project and how to present that knowledge to others.

Lucy: But do we want to do a book instead of an exhibit? Or do we want to do both? Can we do both?

Tricia: I don't really mind doin' the exhibit now 'cause I'm quite proud of the fact that I have them pictures picked out and am writin' about 'em.

Winnie: How does everyone else feel about their photographs, though?

Nóra: I was feelin' horrible about 'em yesterday. So much has changed in my life this year, and when I reviewed the photos when we were putting them on the wall, I wanted to cry. Wanted to throw them all away. But then we talked about it and we talked about how pictures capture a particular time and place and that's what so powerful about them. They don't tell the whole story, or the best part of a story, or the worst part of a story. But they do tell one part of the story. So, I'm OK with them now. But I don't know if I want to do the exhibit just yet. Maybe the book?

Tricia: I don't know. I'd like to do the exhibit. Just a photograph here and there and a wee bit of writing underneath them. That's the way I'd like it done.

Sorcha: But if we did a book, we could have an introduction and go on about times where we would be in each other's company a lot and where there's trust and support and even when ya don't see these people, ya know they're there for ya. We can't get all that information in if we do an exhibit.

Patricia: I like that idea, too. But couldn't we put some of that information in the exhibit?

Winnie: But Sorcha's right. In a book, we could get more stuff in, and then we could have different sections with our photographs instead of each of us having our own individual panels in the exhibit.

Jacqueline: Let's do the exhibit and see what people think.

Winnie: But it doesn't matter what people think, does it?

Deirdre: The reason I want to do the exhibit is 'cause a book is something you buy. But you put your photos in an exhibit, and it's open to people. People don't have to pay to see the exhibit. Anyone can come. Unless that's not what you all want.

Sorcha: That's why I think a book is better. Too many people lookin' at us if we do the exhibit.

(laughter)

Winnie: I agree with that, too. Depends on my mood. When I'm feelin' good about the photos, I want an exhibit. When I'm feelin' like my life here is doin' my head in, I want the book.

(crosstalk)

Deirdre: But if we do the exhibit, anybody can come in and take something from it and go, "Oh, yeah. I felt like that one there," or "That makes me think about this," or "That's such a nice picture." But you make a conscious decision to pick up a book about women in a community in Belfast who did a project together. An exhibit would be more open to everyone.

Lucy: Yeah, that's a good point. A lot of people think that the Monument Road community is all about the Orange marches[1] and nothing else. They don't see that we do lots of other things, like with the kids and the recreation center.

Deirdre: We feel good about what we're doin' now in the project. It took us a while, Alice, but we do. We're glad we took the photos and we can express what we want to say by writing about them. I'm sure that people have a bunch of ideas about women in Belfast, and so these photos tell things about our lives that people don't know. There are some people who are in the same boat as us, and our photos might help them, just like they've helped us to see ourselves differently in some ways.

Winnie: Can we see how the photo exhibit would look, like can we lay it out somehow and then also look at how a book might look and then decide?

Patricia: Yeah, maybe we could see what other people have done and then decide what to do. (October 27, 2001)

I agreed to show the women a number of books that reflected different types of projects in which participants used photographs and texts to convey a message to others. I also asked them if they would like me to invite my friend who worked with the young people in Bridgeport to come to Belfast during my next visit and discuss what a photo-text exhibit might look like. The women agreed that viewing books and meeting someone who could assist them in their decision-making process would be a valuable contribution to them and to the overall project.

Therefore, during my next visit to Belfast, I brought a number of books for the women to peruse. I also brought my friend, who brought a new set of eyes to the women's work. She asked thoughtful questions, offered comments and suggestions to the women about how they might create a photo-text exhibit, and most important, expressed her admiration for the work they had already done.

The ways in which my friend invited the women to reframe and clarify how they could present their work in a photo-text exhibit provided them with a new sense of confidence in themselves and a renewed enthusiasm for designing an exhibit. It was by engaging in discussions with my friend that the women finally decided to first create a photo-text exhibit and then, if the desire was still there, to develop some kind of manuscript that would include additional material not conducive to the completed exhibit.

Arriving at the point where the women agreed to display their photographs and texts "for all the world to see" (Tricia) was a challenging one. They disagreed about how many photographs to use; how to analyze the photographs; how to craft the writings that accompanied the photographs; how to identify themselves in the exhibit (e.g., nationalists, republicans, women living in Belfast, Monument Road women, and/or Catholic); and, as important, how much of their lives they would reveal to outsiders.

Yet the disagreements and the variety of perspectives the women held about certain issues were necessary ingredients in their process of coming to understand how to frame the photo-text exhibit. Ultimately, the women succeeded in presenting themselves, and their work, in ways that respected their individual wishes and demonstrated their collective pride in aspects of the Monument Road community.

Collectively agreeing to display the photo-text exhibit was a breakthrough for the women. Their decision to move outside the conference room, take pride in the value of what they had to say, and present themselves to various groups of outsiders was an action that came as a result of the cyclical process of PAR, providing the women with the opportunity to inform "people like us and people not like us what our lives are *really* like" (Lucy).

In August 2002, the women's photo-text exhibit was displayed at the West Belfast Festival. It was an exciting experience for all of us. Standing in the room where the exhibit was displayed provided us with the opportunity to see, feel, and touch the results of a 2-year process of exploration, reflection, and action. The visceral response the women had to their work deepened their appreciation for and understanding of their everyday lives. As important, the women were able to present aspects of their lives that are in sharp contrast to how their life experiences are often perceived by outsiders. Although the women realize that there is some validity to the perception that Monument Road can be a violence-prone area, they also recognize that Monument Road is a place that connotes safety, action, freedom, potentiality, and a sensation of coming to life (Tuan, 1999). Through their photographs and words, they succeeded in transmitting that message to others, who, we hope, will benefit from their work.

CONCLUDING REFLECTIONS

As the above data reveal, an important aspect of PAR is that participants do not take action on everything that is brought to light in a collaborative project. There is an ebb and flow in PAR projects. Thus, there are times when people are energized and feel a deep need to act on a particular issue. There are also times when people are less enthusiastic about taking a particular action. Sometimes, that is because an action requires a degree of energy that participants either do not possess or choose not to use at a particular historical moment. Other times, participants hesitate to act on an issue because they are uncertain of the implications the action might have for them and their communities. The participants' uncertainty is an important element to consider because as Kemmis and McTaggart (2005) suggest, participants in PAR projects must be willing to "reasonably live with the consequences of the decisions they make, and the actions they take, and the actions that follow from these decisions" (p. 578).

Although the women struggled with the implications of revealing aspects of their lives to people outside the Monument Road community, they also realized that by sharing their experiences in a public way, they could assist other people who are experiencing, or have experienced, similar situations and events. They were willing to live with the decisions they made in terms of displaying their photographs, realizing that their decision had a positive effect on them, their community, and the hundreds of people who have viewed their work.

Similarly, the young people realized that once they made the decision to organize the cleanup event, and to go public with it, they needed to take the actions necessary to accomplish event-related goals. For the most part, they accepted their responsibilities as members of an active group of people willing "to go the extra step to pitch in and make our community better lookin' than it is right now" (Monique).

As the data reveal, action, in and of itself, does not confer on participants of PAR projects the power to change policy. In the case of the young people and the women, their actions did not alleviate the social injustices that frame their lives. Yet what the participants did do was respond in humanizing and authentic ways to issues that concerned them. By doing so, they concretized local knowledge and used that knowledge to make change.

NOTE

1. There are over 3,000 Orange marches throughout the North of Ireland during the summer months. For many years, two of those marches occurred in the Monument Road community—one on July 12th and the other on August 12th. July 12th is the annual Protestant celebration commemorating the victory of William of Orange over the Catholic King James II in 1689. August 12th is a major celebration for the Apprentice Boys, an organization of Protestant men who gather to march in commemoration of the day when 13 Apprentice Boys closed the gates of Derry, keeping King James and his forces from taking over the city. (The British government and many Protestants, unionists, and loyalists refer to the city of Derry as Londonderry. Catholics, nationalists, and republicans refer to the city as Derry.)

4

WHAT CONSTITUTES "RESEARCH" IN PARTICIPATORY ACTION RESEARCH?

Since PAR leads researchers into previously unfamiliar pathways, involvement in the process is likely to stimulate us to think in new ways about old and new theoretical problems, thus generating provocative new ideas.

(Whyte, Greenwood, & Lazes, 1989, p. 538)

How participant groups move from exploring aspects of their lives, their communities, and their concerns to presenting knowledge of their exploration and analysis to outsiders is unique to each group. That is because no two PAR projects are the same. The activities, methods, participants, objectives, and collection techniques are all particular to the context in which the project takes place.

The fact that PAR is context specific means that practitioners draw on a variety of quantitative, qualitative, and creative-based methods to engage participants in the construction of knowledge—for example, surveys, interviews, focus groups, mapping, dramatization, movement, theater, symbolic art, and photovoice (see Chapter Two). Owing to the diversity of the methods used, there is also a diversity of analytical methods utilized by researchers and participants to analyze research data.

In the Belfast and Bridgeport projects, we used photographs, paintings, collages, interviews, and group dialogue to make meaning of the women's and the young people's experiences. As the data reveal, both participant groups used various analytical approaches to synthesize the data they generated in their respective projects.

The approaches the participants used to research project-related issues were linked to the questions that guided both PAR processes. As in most

PAR projects, the initial research questions lead to the emergence of new questions and new avenues of inquiry, all of which *informed* the research process rather than *demanded* that it flow a certain way.

Below, I list some of the questions that were generated in the two projects described herein. I do so to illustrate the extent to which PAR processes generate countless questions that may not be easily or quickly answered but that, if deemed important, are researched in ways that benefit those involved.

- What do you perceive as a problem or an issue in your community that needs to be addressed?
- How does it relate to your life? To the community's life?
- Why do these issues/problems exist?
- What can we do about them?
- What do we need to know?
- What do we already know?
- What resources do we need to proceed with the project?
- How will this project benefit the participants and the rest of the community?
- What are the common themes that have been generated in the research process?
- How do we summarize these themes in ways that benefit those involved?
- Who will control the research project? Make the decisions? Decide how to disseminate information to others?
- How will we address issues of confidentiality and privacy in the dissemination of the information we gather in the project?
- How will we inform others about the project?
- Will our research represent only the realities of those involved or those of other members of the community/group as well?
- What are the criteria we will use to assess the adequacy and efficacy of the project?

The process of addressing the above questions generated research data that became a rich source of knowledge for the young people and the women and assisted them in concretizing aspects of their PAR projects. Owing to age, level of understanding of the analysis process, and confidence in questioning data, the young people and the women analyzed the knowledge they generated in their own particular ways. In this chapter, I discuss how the participant groups and I engaged in processes of reviewing, discussing, summarizing, and analyzing research data. I describe how taking control of the knowledge that was produced through questioning and critical dialogue strengthened the participants' abilities to speak to and about their daily lives.

"YOU SHOULD WRITE STUFF THAT SHOWS PEOPLE WHAT WE CAN DO"

One tool that assisted the participant groups and me in assessing project-related data was the transcripts of the group sessions. The transcripts were collective products owned by each group, not "data" that belonged primarily to me. Thus, they were important tools that supported critical reflection and facilitated critical awareness among those involved (Chiu, 2003). I transcribed all the group sessions and on an ongoing basis reviewed and discussed the transcripts with both participant groups. During that process, we also developed analytical strategies for determining the most salient features of the participants' dialogue.

The young people's first experience analyzing data came when I asked them if they wanted to present their work to faculty and students at the university where I worked. They were eager to do so, yet they realized that to represent themselves and what they were doing in the project effectively, they needed to review "tons of stuff and say it right so we don't sound stupid in front of people" (Blood). I asked them how they wanted to review the "tons of stuff" that was generated in the project thus far.

Rebecca: Why don't we read through all the stuff we've said so far and the stuff we've already done? You always bring the tapes with you right, and then you type them out and have the papers, too, right?

Alice: Right.

Flanango: That'll take too long.

Jeter: We could listen to the tapes.

Flanango: That'll take too long, too.

Tee: Well, ya know how we break into groups sometimes to do stuff. We could break into groups and each group can read some of the group stuff. Then we can tell each other what we think is important to say.

Janine: Yeah, that's a good idea. Let's do that.

Collin: But what if we all come up with different stuff? I mean, we're not presenting all day.

Alice: True. You'll have about twenty minutes, and then we'll have a question-and-answer session where the audience will have a chance to ask you questions about the project.

Blood: Forget it. I'm not doin' it if they get to ask me questions. What if I don't know an answer?

Mase: One of us will know the answer.

Blood: How do you know?

Alice: I understand your hesitancy, Blood, but I would not worry about that right now. Let's decide how you would like to present the work you have done so far, and then we'll discuss the overall event.

(crosstalk)

Tonesha: OK, let's do it. Sometimes we talk so much about things we run out of time to do anything. (April, 3, 1998)

During the next session, we broke into four groups. Each group was joined by a member of the research team who acted as a coparticipant and assisted the young people in summarizing and analyzing the group dialogue. Previous to forming the groups, we discussed how we would review and synthesize the data in the transcripts. After brainstorming a variety of ideas, we decided to frame our reviews of the transcripts around three questions:

1. What are the major issues, questions, and concerns that we see in the transcripts?

2. What message do we want to convey to the audience as a result of reviewing the data?

3. How do we want to convey that message?

Over the course of the next three sessions, the young people and the university-based team reviewed over 25 transcripts. Each group reviewed a particular set of transcripts and highlighted topics that they believed needed to be addressed in the presentation. Then they summarized the topics and brainstormed ways to effectively communicate their concerns about those topics to others. For example, one of the groups reviewed a number of transcripts that contained discussions about the collages the young people created at the beginning of the project. (The collages were one of the tools that we used to better understand how the young people defined their community. See McIntyre, 2000.)

The participants' collages included images of sports, guns, drugs, career possibilities, music, education, and their neighborhoods. The discussions that ensued as a result of the collages ranged from the community being negatively affected by drugs, guns, violence, and "too much trash," to the community being a place where nice people live, where families grow up together, where young people play sports, and where people develop friendships with one another.

The group that reviewed the transcripts related to the collages decided that they needed to present aspects of those collages to the university audience. They specifically wanted to inform audience members that there were "good parts of the community and bad parts of the community." They wanted to show the audience that they enjoyed playing sports and "hanging out with our friends." Yet they also wanted to convey a serious message to the audience: that there was too much violence in their community, and they wanted it to stop. The group then decided that an effective way to convey that message was to speak about the issues at the same time that they showed the audience photographs of the completed collages. In that way, they could illuminate the themes the collages generated in the group discussions.

The three remaining groups engaged in similar review processes. They, too, reviewed a number of participant-generated discussions in the transcripts that focused on violence, "too much trash," and drug abuse in the community. The participants in those groups also highlighted topics that they wanted to include in the presentation: education, the need the young people have to "make something" of themselves, and the participants' desires to have successful careers when they reach adulthood.

After each group reviewed their sets of transcripts, we came together, reviewed each group's summary, and began the process of framing an agreed-upon presentation based on the themes that the young people extracted from the data. The final presentation included references to the four main issues that the participants repeatedly questioned, discussed, and sought information about in the group sessions: violence in the community owing to guns and drugs; the need for a good education; the poor state of the environment; and the importance of family, friends, and community.

The participants developed a comprehensive presentation that reflected their understanding of the issues they had discussed in their group sessions. By analyzing the research materials they were able to highlight the most salient aspects of the project for an outside audience. In addition, their analysis generated questions, themes, and ideas that were later used to move the project forward.

"WE INVENTED OUR OWN WAY OF MAKING SENSE OF IT ALL"

Like the young people, the women reviewed their session transcripts, as well as the data they generated as a result of engaging in other project-related activities (e.g., clay stories, painting, and collages). They, too, broke into small groups, reviewed the transcripts, and generated a number of themes that they felt represented the multiple discussions they engaged in during the project: family and community, violence, gender and war, politics, education, and what it means to be a woman living in the North of Ireland.

Once they agreed on the themes they had generated in the group discussions, the women began the process of reviewing and analyzing their photographs. Like the participants in the Bridgeport project, the women and I generated a number of questions to assist them as they initiated the photo-analysis process. Yet, in contrast to how the young people's questions helped them to analyze their texts and photographs, the questions we formulated for the women constrained that process (see Chapter Two). They found the questions "too confusing." Therefore, the women "invented our own way of making sense of it all" (Lucy). What they "invented" was a process in which they *individually* chose photographs to reflect the themes they had previously agreed on *collectively* (see above). The women clearly decided that the most important factor to consider in their analysis was what the photographs *meant* to them individually rather than how their photographs fit into the framework they developed by analyzing the session transcripts. By deciding to proceed in this way, the women felt more confident in linking their interpretations of the photographs and the group dialogues to the collective action of designing and displaying a photo-text exhibit representing their individual and collective lives.

PRACTITIONERS AND THE DATA-ANALYSIS PROCESS

It is my belief that practitioners of PAR have an obligation *at the beginning* of a PAR project to let their desires be known to research participants about how they, as researchers, intend to analyze and disseminate research data. That is because participants are the stakeholders of project-related data and therefore should determine its use and the conditions for its publication and dissemination at every stage of the research process (Fals-Borda, 1987).

Therefore, at the onset of each project and at various times throughout both PAR projects, I explained to the participant groups that one aspect of my participation in the project was the attention I paid to summarizing, analyzing, and critiquing the data so as to present aspects of the projects to various community groups, as well as academic audiences, such as students, colleagues, researchers, educators, and psychologists. Those presentations would include articles, books, conference proceedings, and informal discussions in the classes I teach. I told both groups that I would inform them of what I intended to write or speak about prior to doing so and that they would have opportunities to question my representations of the projects. I also told them that if they preferred that I *not* present aspects of their work to others, I would honor their decisions.

It is my experience that *talking* about how one's life will be presented in published work and then actually *seeing* one's life on paper are two different experiences and engender different sets of feelings and responses. One way that I brought those two experiences together for the participant groups was to show them drafts of manuscripts I was writing so they could get an idea of how their lives were presented in written form. In those manuscripts, I highlighted the themes that I generated from the data.

In both projects, I used social constructionist grounded theory method to analyze the group data. Social constructionist grounded theory provides a framework for "developing conceptual categories [that] arise through our interpretations *of* data rather than *from* them" (Charmaz, 2005, p. 509; italics in the original). In addition, it encourages researchers to be reflexive about how "their prior interpretive frames, biographies, and interests as well as the research context, their relationships with research participants, concrete field experiences, and modes of generating and recording empirical materials" (p. 509) influence their analysis.

I chose to use social constructionist grounded theory method because of my familiarity with the method (see McIntyre, 2000; 2004). I was confident that it was an effective, valid, and representative approach for analyzing multivocal group dialogue. Throughout both research processes, I listened to the audiotapes of the group meetings and identified themes, categories, and concepts that were generated in the group dialogues. I then offered these as reflections to the participants, inviting them to clarify, elaborate on, and critique my interpretations.

I analyzed the data regarding various forms of violence in the context of the larger discourse about the war in the North of Ireland. Although the women appreciated the link between their everyday experiences and existing scholarship about women and war, they "skimmed over the academic stuff you wrote and went right for what it was *we* said. And we hated readin' what we said. We sound like we're full of shite" (Deirdre). "Yeah," Winnie said, "we hate seein' ourselves on the paper like that."

Nevertheless, the women realized that many people living outside of Belfast have a distorted and stereotypical view of what life is like for the people living there. In addition, the women knew that their experiences growing up and living through a 35-year war might benefit others. Therefore, the women's overall response was, "If someone has to blabber on about us, it might was well be you, Alice" (Deirdre). "Yeah, you have our permission to write on and on about us, Alice. We trust ya, and give you our blessins' as ya take us across the ocean and put us in a book" (Tricia).

Presenting the young people with drafts of the manuscripts I was writing was more of a challenge. Understandably, the academic discourse that my analysis and interpretation was embedded in was difficult for them to comprehend. Therefore, I summarized the topics, themes, and ideas that I was writing about to the young people, informing them about how I was presenting various aspects of their dialogues in print. Usually, the young people nodded politely and told me that they trusted what I wrote about the project and about how the project was linked to issues like education, racism, and violence. Like the women, the young people were not exactly interested in what I had to say about certain issues; rather, they were interested in what *they* had to say and whether "they sounded stupid."

I assured them that, indeed, they did not sound stupid. On the contrary, I informed them that they sounded like young people grappling with a number of issues in ways that led to constructive change. I then showed them various pieces of group dialogue that I was using in my writings. Once they saw those, they realized that they did not "sound stupid." Therefore, they informed me that as long as I did not make them "look dumb, we have no problem with you writin' about us" (Mase).

In addition to my familiarity with social constructionist grounded theory, a second factor informed my data analysis: integrating the *participants'* interpretations about their research-related experiences to academic scholarship. I paid close attention to the photographs and texts the young people chose and crafted for their photo-text exhibit. I also integrated the texts they crafted for the multiple presentations they conducted into my analysis and linked them to the issues noted earlier (e.g., urban education, racism, and violence). In addition, I integrated the participants' interpretations of their collages, storytelling exercises, and one-to-one interviews into the overall analysis so as to demonstrate how the young people made meaning of the multiple issues generated in the project.

I took a similar approach with the women. In my analysis and in my writings, I attended to the categories the women generated from the project-related activities and the group dialogue, often contextualizing them in the larger discourse about the war in the North of Ireland. In addition, I revealed aspects of the women's meaning-making by integrating their interpretations of their photographs, clay figures, storytelling, watercolor paintings, and one-to-one interviews into the overall analysis.

The final factor that informed my analysis was my relationship with the work of other practitioners of participatory action research. Like me, many practitioners of PAR are eager to learn from others about how to effectively engage in PAR projects. They question each another, critique each other's projects, borrow certain tools and techniques from one another, gather together at conferences to listen and learn, collaborate in publishing scholarship related to PAR, and engage in ongoing communication with one another so as to expand the field of participatory action research. Therefore, I relied heavily (and still do) on the writings of practitioners of PAR as I crafted manuscripts and presentations about the Bridgeport and Belfast projects.

The approach I used to analyze data from both projects did not completely reflect the horizontal equality I strived for between the participants and me in terms of analyzing multiple data sources. As Harding and Norberg (2005) suggest, in spite of feminists' heroic attempts to eliminate the power differences in terms of writing up and representing research, "this goal has proved impossible" (p. 2012). Yet, as they further argue, there are "better and worse ways" (p. 2012) for researchers to address those issues. In terms of the young people and the women, the fact that neither group had been formally instructed in how to analyze data influenced to what extent they would and could collaborate in the data analysis. Yet that did not mean that the participants were absent from the analysis process. They were active participants to the extent that they chose to be or could be. In both cases, I felt confident that we had found a "better" way, rather than a "worse" one, to effectively represent their lives to others.

REPRESENTING MULTIPLE PERSPECTIVES

There was an effort made by all those involved in the Belfast and Bridgeport projects to make room for multiple perspectives, both in the group sessions and in the public documents and presentations that came as a result of the projects. That is because the knowledge that is generated and disseminated in a PAR project does not always support all of the participants' ideas, objectives, and goals.

As the data reveal, there were times when the participant groups disagreed about strategies for moving their projects in a particular direction. Most times, those disagreements were worked out, although not necessarily to everyone's satisfaction. If those disagreements were internal to the group and were going to remain there, they tended to "sort themselves out" as the women would say. For example, sometimes the young people disagreed about who would take responsibility for certain tasks, and those disagreements were internal. The discussions that ensued between and among the participants about how to resolve the issue of who would do what were significant aspects of the collaborative process. Yet it was not an issue that would distort the reality of the project or confuse outsiders if it were revealed in a presentation, manuscript, book, or photo-text exhibit. On the other hand, an issue that is both internal *and* external can be challenging for participants to negotiate. For example, as noted in Chapter Three, the women disagreed about whether they should be identified in any publication or presentation as nationalists, republicans, Catholics, or simply women living in Belfast. The women's identities as nationalists or republicans, Sinn Fein supporters or supporters of a different political party, supporters of the current peace process, or women who disagree with a number of concessions that were made to achieve peace, are significant aspects of their individual and collective lives. Sometimes, the differences in their identities were muted under their collective identities as victims of the war. Other times, those differences were highlighted and needed to be addressed, accepted, and integrated into how the data were presented and disseminated to outsiders. By making room for multiple perspectives, the women succeeded in presenting themselves and their work in ways that respected their individual identities and at the same time demonstrated their collective identity as women of the Monument Road community.

It is also important that practitioners of PAR address participants' multiple perspectives in *their* representations of research projects to outside audiences. Multiple perspectives may mean multiple interpretations. Therefore, practitioners need to find ways to integrate contradictory perspectives into any academic-based manuscript they produce while simultaneously presenting the threads of continuity and agreement that maintained and sustained the project over time.

CONCLUDING REFLECTIONS

As Kemmis and McTaggart (2005) argue, "What makes participatory action research 'research' is not the machinery of research techniques"

(p. 574). Rather, they suggest that research in the context of PAR is more about building a relationship between theory and practice. As important, "it involves learning about real, material, concrete, and particular practices of particular people in particular places" (p. 564).

It was by revisiting the participants' practices, as well as their life experiences, both during group discussions and also through various stages of analysis and interpretation, that the young people and the women were given the opportunity to view themselves and their concerns from new and different perspectives. Once reviewed, revisited, analyzed, and articulated, the participants were able to make the results of their research projects available to the public. In so doing, the young people and the women provided evidence to others that their research was data driven, credible, accurate, and trustworthy. In addition, their efforts demonstrated that a collective will to make individual and collective change can occur in collaborative research processes. Sometimes the change comes quickly, sometimes slowly. It is my experience that some kind of change will always materialize if practitioners and participants work for it.

5

CONCLUDING REFLECTIONS

> PAR is a philosophy of life as much as a method, a sentiment
> as much as a conviction.
>
> (Fals-Borda, 1997, p. 111)

In this chapter, I review a number of factors that were threaded throughout
both PAR projects. First, I discuss how participants and researchers assess
the "success" and/or "failure" of a PAR project. I argue that participants
and practitioners of PAR need to be cautious about how we judge "victory"
and "defeat" within the context of participatory action research. Second, I
revisit some of the ethical issues that arise in PAR projects. Given the
processual nature of PAR, ethical issues arise at different points in the
research process. Therefore, practitioners of PAR need to ensure that ethical questions are integrated into each phase of the project. Similarly, they
need to include participants in that integration, thus providing them with
opportunities to take responsibility for participating in a conscientious,
trustworthy, and ethical process. Finally, I discuss the implications of participatory action research. In so doing, I invite others to consider PAR as an
approach for working with people in processes of change so as to improve
the contexts in which they live.

DEFINING "SUCCESS" AND "FAILURE" IN PAR

Reason (1993) reminds us that PAR "takes place within a community of
inquiry which is capable of effective communication and self-reflection"
(p. 1268). This self-reflection is not a license for "anything goes." Rather,
self-reflection, in conjunction with investigation, critical questioning, dialogue, generative activities, and a determination to take action about issues
under exploration, contributes to the development of a project that is judged

not against the criterion of an objective truth but against the criterion of whether the people involved are better off because of their experiences as participants in a PAR project. When PAR projects are assessed in that light, people can, with confidence, "put [their] trust . . . in the human process of critical curiosity" (p. 1268) and take responsibility for the highs, lows, successes, and failures that result from a collaborative effort to effect change.

"WE'LL JUST THINK OF SOMETHIN' ELSE TO DO"

In the third year of the project, the young people presented the information they gathered regarding the state of the environment to members of the Bridgeport city council. They requested that the city council do three things: create a task force to address the environment; make a commitment to give time, energy, and resources to inform the public about cleaning up the environment; and place more trash receptacles in particular locations in Bridgeport.

The city council was impressed with the young people's work and promised them that they "would absolutely put more trash receptacles in the community" and would assist them in any way they could in fulfilling their goals.

Weeks went by, and we failed to hear from any member of the city council regarding the young people's proposal. Therefore, the participants wrote letters and made multiple telephone calls to city council members. Again, we failed to get a response. At that point, I decided to call certain government officials and inquire as to why they had failed to respond to the young people's efforts to clean up the community. After numerous telephone conversations, I was told by a representative of the city council that "the city couldn't just put trash bins everywhere and do public service announcements without a budget, and there was no budget for this."

I reminded the representative that the city council had promised the young people that they would address the issues they brought before them. The representative's response was that as far as she was concerned, the council would not be taking any action to address the young people's concerns.

I informed the participants about my conversation with the representative to the city council. Unfortunately, they were not surprised. Yet rather than give up on their efforts to effect change in the community, the participants responded with the suggestion that they move forward with the project *without* the city's assistance.

Tee: We'll do it, anyway. We can just get people involved some other way.

Melinda: We did it so far without them, so we can do it some more.

Risha: Yeah, that doesn't mean we have to stop tryin'. We're dedicated.

Tonesha: So if they don't help us, we'll just think of somethin' else to do. (September 27, 1999)

The young people *did* think of other things to do. They contacted a reporter for a local newspaper. They presented their experiences in the project to the reporter and explained the lack of support from the city council. The reporter followed up on her discussion with the participants by contacting members of the city council. Shortly thereafter, the reporter published an article explaining the participants' project and the city council's response to the young people's requests for city resources. The publication of the article resulted in a number of responses from various community groups, some of whom ultimately joined the young people in their efforts to organize a communitywide event.

The young people never did get the trash receptacles they were promised. Nor did the city council take action on the participants' two other requests. Yet the young people did not experience the city council's lack of action as a failure on *their* part. Rather, they viewed the lack of action by the council as a failure on the *council's* part. In their eyes, the council members "made a big mistake not helpin' us because our cleanup event was a big success, better than we imagined. Now they don't get to have any of the credit" (Risha).

"SORRY WE FAILED TO GET IT ALL DONE, ALICE"

One of the main reasons the women of Belfast decided to go forth with presenting the culmination of their project to outsiders was that they hoped their photo stories would help other people who lived through similar experiences or who were unaware of the realities that structure people's lives during a war. Therefore, during one of my visits to Belfast, the women and I collaborated in the writing of a funding proposal that would assist us in taking the photo-text exhibit to a variety of communities throughout the North of Ireland.

I returned to the United States shortly after we completed the majority of the writing. We agreed that the women would complete the final steps: finalize things at the bank, secure the signature of the director of the community center, and send the completed application to the appropriate agency.

Two months later, and after numerous long-distance telephone conversations, Lucy informed me that the women were preoccupied with other community-related issues and thus had "failed to get it all done, Alice."

I was disappointed that we missed the opportunity to secure additional funding for the project and viewed missing the grant deadline as a failure. The women saw the situation differently. "It's not really a failure, Alice. The peace agreement—that's a failure. This was just a missed deadline" (Lucy). As Lucy's comments suggest, viewing success and failure is contextual and mediated by the circumstances and situations that are particular to the participants and the conditions under which they live. Completing a grant was not a priority for the women in the light of other war-related and community-based issues that had to be addressed in their lives.

My experience with the women "failing to get it done" reminded me that, as Kemmis and Wilkinson (1998) suggest, success is not based on whether participants complete "the steps faithfully, but whether they have a strong and authentic sense of development and evolution" (p. 21) stemming from their participation in a PAR project. The women in Belfast *did* have a strong sense that what they were doing authentically represented their lives and that their work had evolved into "a brilliant display of the women on the Road" (Sorcha). They did not need to complete a grant proposal to confirm that.

Both the Belfast and Bridgeport projects demonstrate that engaging in participatory processes of change is difficult to assess, particularly when those processes challenge people to think differently, act differently, and take actions without the certainty of "success." Yet it is precisely the unexpected twists and turns that occur in ongoing collaborative processes that generate creative energy, increase the possibility of people becoming agents of change in their own lives, and make it necessary for practitioners and participants to find various ways to evaluate success. Some of those evaluations cannot be concretized into measurable form. As Cooper (2005) argues, "While some gains are measurable, who can put a value on the opportunity to work for something you believe in? Or estimate the psychological impact of witnessing your words move and motivate people to join you in an attempt at change?" (p. 474)

Success came about in the two PAR projects because it raised awareness in the minds of those involved. That raising of awareness moved outside the groups and benefited people in the participants' respective communities—people who might otherwise be unaware that there was a solution to a particular problem or a particular way to view a community issue. In addition, the participants developed abilities that assisted them in conducting research, enhanced their knowledge about their local environment, and increased their skills as advocates for social change (Boser, 2006). Similarly, the young people and the women experienced success by developing a "more positive sense of self, greater sensitivity to the needs of others, [and] increased understanding of democratic values and behaviours" (Cooper, 2005, p. 473).

However limited the young people's and the women's "success" might have been within their respective projects, their actions reflected their desires and how they wanted to see their stories brought to life. As important, both groups succeeded in producing histories about themselves and their particular experiences that might not have been produced if they had not transformed their knowledge and understanding into concrete actions.

ETHICAL ISSUES IN PARTICIPATORY ACTION RESEARCH

As noted in Chapter One and in other sections of this book, the ethical dimensions of PAR projects are of paramount importance if practitioners and participants are to effectively work together for change. Owing to the longevity of many PAR projects, the relationships that develop between participants and practitioners lead to a different set of ethical challenges than those that arise in traditional social science research projects. Therefore, at the onset of each project, I reviewed a number of ethical issues with the participants—for example, informed consent, documentation of data, ownership of data, control of the overall PAR process, confidentiality, privacy, trustworthiness, and responsibility. The participant groups and I continued to discuss those issues many times throughout the PAR projects.

We also discussed the potential risk to the participants in relation to some of the issues that might be generated in the research process. I informed the women, as well as the young people and their parents and caregivers, that I would be attentive to the participants' comfort levels and accompany them through any discomfort that may occur as a result of reflecting on particular issues. In addition, I informed them that we would be engaging in ongoing discussions throughout the projects regarding the participants' sense of safety and security within a collaborative group setting.

I also invited the participants to join me in specifying procedures with respect to their anonymity and the confidentiality of their responses. I requested that both groups collaborate with me in changing identifying indicators that would reveal information about who they were, where they lived, and what they said and did during the projects. In response, we changed the names of some people, places, and things in Belfast and Bridgeport. Some of the women chose their own pseudonyms that were used throughout the project. Others, like Patricia, "refuse to use any other name than my own, so just put me down with my real name." All of the young people who participated in the project chose their own pseudonyms that were used throughout the research project.

Informed consent posed a different challenge, particularly in the Bridgeport project. Owing to the fact that the young people were minors, and attending school during the project, I first received permission from the principal of the Blair School to initiate the overall process. I then obtained parents' and caregivers' permission for their children's participation in the project. Following that, I provided an initial consent form to the young people and their families—a form that we modified as the project evolved and the activities changed. The modified consent forms were necessary because, as Boser (2006) suggests, "Participants cannot be given informed consent to research activities in advance, because the full scope of the process of the research is not determined in advance . . . . [They are] typically negotiated by participants at each stage of the research cycle" (p. 12).

In addition, I notified both participant groups that I would take responsibility for storing the data that were generated in the projects. All collected written data, audiotapes, and participant-produced items would be kept by me. I also informed the groups that, at their request, the data would be available for them to review, discuss, and, if necessary, revisit as a group.

Privacy, confidentiality, anonymity, minimizing risks, preventing exposure to danger, and ensuring a safe context for individual and collective reflection and action cannot be assured in a PAR project. This is attributable, in part, to the fact that people are social beings and thus cannot be restrained from either intentionally or unintentionally speaking about their life experiences to people outside the PAR process. In addition, PAR is an open, dialectical process that extends beyond the site of the project. People's perspectives about the research experience, the knowledge they gained, and the actions they took may be articulated in a host of ways privately or publicly. Furthermore, it may be impossible to modify identifying information to the degree that the location of the project, and all those involved, is guaranteed.

Nonetheless, practitioners of PAR must do their best to apply ethical principles and invite participants to assist them in balancing the many different elements of a PAR process. In so doing, both parties have a vested interest in addressing agreed-upon goals in an atmosphere of trust and reciprocity.

IMPLICATIONS OF PARTICIPATORY ACTION RESEARCH

There are many contributions that PAR makes to social science research. Below, I briefly state three of them. I focus on the contributions of PAR, rather than its inherent challenges, because the challenges of engaging in PAR are necessary elements in participatory processes aimed at change. I suggest that the challenging elements in PAR be viewed not as impediments to the research process but as opportunities for constructing new knowledge and developing new ways of integrating theory, practice, and people's everyday experiences.

One aspect of PAR that makes it significant to social science research is that it is a research approach that is a theory of possibility rather than a theory of predictability (Wadsworth, 1998). Thus, PAR provides multiple opportunities for practitioners and participants to construct knowledge and integrate theory and practice in ways that are unique and practical to a particular group. Working within the context of possibility, those involved in PAR "regard their research practices as a matter of borrowing, constructing, and reconstructing research methods and techniques to throw light on the nature, processes, and consequences of the particular object they are studying" (Kemmis & McTaggart, 2005, p. 575). When research is viewed from this perspective, there is an overall demystification of what research is and how it can relate to people's lives. Participants of PAR projects discover an appreciation of local knowledge and of their capacity to speak about and to that knowledge. In so doing, they enrich their sense of themselves as contributing members of society. That enrichment fosters community-building, and community-building fosters a willingness to engage in ongoing processes of action and change.

A second contribution that PAR makes is that it provides opportunities for people to insert themselves into the research process as subjects of their own history (Freire, 1971). In the projects described herein, both participant groups revealed aspects of their living histories in ways that reflected their personal and collective truths and realities. Neither group assumed that their versions of reality, or their versions of the truth, were the only ones worth telling. On a number of occasions during the Bridgeport project, one or another of the young people inquired as to whether she or he could invite a friend to join the project. That way, their friends could "see what we're doin' in here" (Jessica). They also wanted to know how their friends and classmates felt about the work they were doing and whether they supported the ideas that were generated in the project. Owing to logistics, class schedules, and the inability of the participants' friends to commit to an ongoing project, the participants ultimately decided "to leave it the way it is. . . . We can keep tellin' them what we're doin' and ask them what they think of our ideas and ask them if they want to help us, but I think who we got now is good" (Melinda).

Similarly, the women in Belfast recognized that their perspectives about war-related violence were in some ways particular to them and to their community. Many women across the North of Ireland identify with one another in terms of how they experienced, for example, house raids, curfews, protests, arrests, and various types of surveillance during the war. Yet those experiences were played out differently depending on the particular community being targeted. Thus, there exist multiple lenses through which to view war-related events in the North of Ireland.

That is the third contribution that PAR makes to social science research: It affords groups of people the freedom to explore and value how *they* experience their individual and collective realities. As important, it provides them with the freedom to be innovative about how they engage that process. For the women and the young people, the innovation came through creative activities and group dialogue. Many times, the group-based activities and accompanying dialogues generated enthusiasm, humor, insight, and a decision to move forward on a particular issue. Other times, the cross-fertilization of ideas and beliefs that occurred in the midst of engaging in various activities, and sometimes challenging discussions, led to disagreements within the groups. Given that the participants were taking a risk traveling into previously unfamiliar territory, the disagreements between individual participants were to be expected. In my experience, many times those disagreements were the catalysts for energizing and dislodging people from the fixed positions they held about certain topics and for assisting them in generating provocative new ideas about how to address and solve important practical problems.

CONCLUDING COMMENTS

Lundy & McGovern (2006) participated in a PAR project with relatives and friends of people living in Belfast who died as a result of the Troubles. Rather than name what they were doing as storytelling, the participants of the project chose to define their narratives as truth-telling. The participants "wanted to hold onto the word and concept of 'truth' rather than relinquish it for what was seen as the less evocative and powerful 'story'" (p. 83). As one of the group member's stated:

> If you are going to have any deep healing you have to get some expression of truth even if it is only my truth. It doesn't have to be your truth. It doesn't have to be a shared truth. But before I can actually be healed I have to feel that somebody's heard my story and if they haven't heard my story then I'm not open to letting it go. (p. 83)

For the women in Belfast and the young people in Bridgeport, presenting their "truths" about their life experiences to each other, to me, and to outside communities was an action that may not have produced healing from the various forms of violence that characterize their lives. Yet what both participants groups *did* do was take actions that addressed agreed-upon goals, exercised varying degrees of agency, threw light on aspects of their communities that otherwise may have gone unexplored, and, overall, contributed to their personal and collective growth.

Engaging in the two PAR projects described here benefited me as well. It provided me with the opportunity to be a field worker, researcher, collaborator, interviewer, participant, interpreter, and agent of change. Embracing those positions enabled me to "stay alongside people for the long haul; [and] to make sure 'my' research [was] genuinely instead 'your' research or 'our' research" (Wadsworth, 2005, p. 422). As important, it gave me the opportunity to enrich my understanding of myself, of the young people and the women I had the privilege to work with, and of the power of joining with others to create knowledge for change.

As Freire (1971) suggests, "To be a good [participatory researcher] means above all to have faith in people; to believe in the possibility that they can create and change things" (p. 62). Believing in possibility creates space for people to reflect on themselves and on the ways in which they engage their worlds. That reflection process can then lead to change—a change that is the product of people's knowledge, experience, and practice.

It is my hope that practitioners of PAR continue to have faith in people, continue to support processes of reflection and change, and continue "to create circumstances in which people can search together collaboratively for more comprehensible, true, authentic, and morally right and appropriate ways of understanding and acting in the world" (Kemmis & McTaggart, 2005, p. 578).

References

American Psychological Association (2001). *Publication manual of the American Psychological Association* (5th ed.). Washington, DC: Author.

Angelou, M. (1994). *Phenomenal women: Four poems celebrating women*. New York: Random House.

Argyris, C., & Schön, D. A. (1989). Participatory action research and action science compared. *American Behavioral Scientist, 32*(5), 612–623.

Atweh, B., Kemmis, S., & Weeks, P. (Eds.). (1998). *Action research in practice: Partnerships for social justice in education*. London: Routledge.

Bell, E. E. (2001). Infusing race into the U.S. discourse on action research. In P. Reason & H. Bradbury (Eds.), *Handbook of action research: Participative inquiry and practice* (pp. 48–58). Thousand Oaks, CA: Sage.

Boog, B. W. (2003). The emancipatory character of action research, its history and the present state of the art. *Journal of Community & Applied Psychology, 13*, 426–438.

Boser, S. (2006). Ethics and power in community-campus partnerships for research. *Action Research 4*(1), 9–21.

Brown, D. (1982). Ambiguities in participatory research. In B. Hall, A. Gillette, & R. Tandon (Eds.), *Creating knowledge: A monopoly?* (pp. 203–209). New Delhi: Society for Participatory Research in Asia.

Brown, L. D., & Tandon, R. (1983). Ideology and political economy in inquiry: Action research and participatory research. *Journal of Applied Behavioral Science, 3*, 277–294.

Brydon-Miller, B. (1993). Breaking down barriers: Accessibility self-advocacy in the disabled community. In P. Park, M. Brydon-Miller, B. Hall, & T. Jackson (Eds.), *Voices of change: Participatory research in the United States and Canada* (pp. 125–144). Toronto: Ontario Institute for Studies in Education.

Brydon-Miller, M., Maguire, P., & McIntyre, A. (2004). *Traveling companions: Feminism, teaching, and action research*. Westport, CT: Praeger.

Burnaford, G., Fischer, J. C., & Hobson, D. (Eds.). (2001). *Teachers doing research: The power of action through inquiry* (2nd ed.). Mahwah, NJ: Lawrence Erlbaum.

Charmaz, K. (2005). Grounded theory in the 21st century: Applications for advancing social justice studies. In N. K. Denzin & Y. S. Lincoln (Eds.), *The Sage handbook of qualitative research* (pp. 507–535). Thousand Oaks, CA: Sage.

Chataway, C. J. (1997). An examination of the constraints on mutual inquiry in a participatory action research project. *Journal of Social Issues, 53*(4), 747–766.

Chataway, C. J. (2001). Negotiating the observer–observed relationship: Participatory action research. In D. Tolman & M. Brydon-Miller (Eds.), *From subjects to subjectivities: A handbook of interpretive and participatory methods* (pp. 239–255). New York: New York University Press.

Chiu, L. F. (2003). Transformational potential of focus group practice in participatory action research. *Action Research, 1*(2), 165–183.

Chrisp, J. (2004). The negotiation of divergent demands when community research is located in the academy: The mother–adolescent son project. In M. Brydon-Miller, P. Maguire, & A. McIntyre (Eds.), *Traveling companions: Feminism, teaching, and action research* (pp. 79–95). Westport, CT: Praeger.

Cochran-Smith, M., & Lytle, S. L. (Eds.). (1993). *Inside/outside: Teacher research and knowledge.* New York: Teachers College Press.

Collins, P. H. (1998). *Fighting words: Black women and the search for justice.* Minneapolis: University of Minnesota Press.

Cooper, E. (2005). What do we know about out-of-school youths? How participatory action research can work for young refugees in camps. *Compare, 35*(4), 463–477.

Cornwall, A., & Jewkes, R. (1995). What is participatory research? *Social Science & Medicine, 41*(12), 1667–1676.

de Wit, T., & Gianotten, V. (1980). Rural training in traditional communities of Peru. In F. Dubell, T. Erasmie, & J. de Vries (Eds.), *Research for the people—Research by the people: Selected papers from the International Forum on Participatory Research in Ljubljana, Yugoslavia* (pp. 131–142). Linkoping, Sweden: Linkoping University, and Amersfoort, Netherlands: S. V. E. The Netherlands Study and Development Center for Adult Education.

Dickson, G., & Green, K. (2001). Participatory action research: Lessons learned with Aboriginal grandmothers. *Health Care for Women International, 22,* 471–482.

Elliott, J. (1991). *Action research for educational change.* Buckingham, UK: Open University Press.

Evans, L. (2002). *Reflective practice in educational research: Developing advanced skills.* New York: Continuum International Publishing Group.

Ewald, W. (2001). *Secret games: Collaborative works with children, 1969–1999.* New York: Scalo.

Fals-Borda, O. (1985). *Knowledge and people's power.* New Delhi: Indian Social Institutes.

Fals-Borda, O. (1987). The application of participatory action-research in Latin America. *International Sociology, 2*(4), 329–347.

Fals-Borda, O. (1997). Participatory action research in Columbia: Some personal reflections. In R. McTaggart (Ed.), *Participatory action research: International contexts and consequences* (pp. 107–112). Albany: State University of New York Press.

Fine, M. (1994). Working the hyphens: Reinventing self and other in qualitative research. In N. K. Denzin & Y. S. Lincoln (Eds.), *Handbook of qualitative research* (pp. 70–82). Thousand Oaks, CA: Sage.

Fine, M., Torre, M. E., Boudin, K., Bowen, I., Clark, J., Hylton, D., et al. (2003). Participatory action research: From within and beyond prison bars. In P. M. Camic, J. E. Rhodes, & L. Yardley (Eds.), *Qualitative research in psychology:*

Expanding perspectives in methodology and design (pp. 173–198). Washington, DC: American Psychological Association.

Freire, P. (1970). *Pedagogy of the oppressed* (M. B. Ramos, Trans.). New York: Seabury Press.

Freire, P. (1971). To the coordinator of the culture circle. *Convergence, 4*(1), 61–62.

Freire, P. (1973). *Education for critical consciousness* (M. B. Ramos, Trans.). New York: Seabury Press.

Freire, P. (1985). *The politics of education: Culture, power, and liberation* (D. Macedo, Trans.). South Hadley, MA: Bergin and Harvey.

Gaventa, J., & Horton, B. D. (1981). A citizen's research project in Appalachia, USA. *Convergence, 14*(3), 30–42.

Greenwood, D. J. (2004). Feminism and action research: Is "resistance" possible and, if so, why is it necessary? In M. Brydon-Miller, P. Maguire, & A. McIntyre (Eds.), *Traveling companions: Feminism, teaching, and action research* (pp. 157–168). Westport, CT: Preager.

Greenwood, D. J., & Levin, M. (1998). *Introduction to action research: Social research for social change.* Thousand Oaks, CA: Sage.

Greenwood, D. J., Whyte, W. F., & Harkavy, I. (1993). Participatory action research as a process and as a goal. *Human Relations, 46*(2), 175–192.

Hall, B. (1977). *Creating knowledge: Breaking the monopoly.* Toronto: Participatory Research Project of the International Council of Adult Educators.

Hall, B. (1981). Participatory research, popular knowledge and power: A personal reflection. *Convergence, 14*(3), 6–17.

Harding, S., & Norberg, K. (2005). New feminist approaches to social science methodologies: An introduction. *Signs: Journal of Women in Culture and Society, 30*(4), 2009–2105.

Harris, C. (1993). Whiteness as property. *Harvard Law Review, 106*(8), 1709–1791.

Heron, J. (1988). Validity in co-operative inquiry. In P. Reason (Ed.), *Human inquiry in action: Developments in new paradigm research* (pp. 40–59). London: Sage.

Hollingsworth, S. (Ed.). (1997). *International action research: A casebook for educational reform.* Washington, DC: Falmer Press.

hooks, b. (2000). *Feminist theory: From margin to center* (2nd ed.). Boston: South End Press.

Jason, L. E., Keys, C. B., Suarez-Balcazar, Y., Taylor, R. R., & Davis, M. I. (Eds.). (2004). *Participatory community research: Theories and methods in action.* Washington, DC: American Psychological Association.

Jackson, T., & McKay, G. (1982). Sanitation and water supply in Big Trout Lake: Participatory research for democratic technical solutions. *Canadian Journal of Native Studies 2*(1), 129–145.

Kanhare, V. P. (1980). The struggle in Dhulia: A women's movement in India. In F. Dubell, T. Erasmie, & J. de Vries (Eds.), *Research for the people—Research by the people: Selected papers from the International Forum on Participatory Research in Ljubljana, Yugoslavia* (pp. 110–117). Linkoping, Sweden:

Linkoping University, and Amersfoort, Netherlands: S. V. E. The Netherlands Study and Development Center for Adult Education.

Kay, C. B. (2003). *The complete guide to service learning: Proven, practiced ways to engage students in civil responsibility, academic curriculum, and social action.* Minneapolis, MN: Free Spirit Publishing.

Kemmis, S. (2001). Exploring the relevance of critical theory for action research: Emancipatory action research in the footsteps of Jürgen Habermas. In P. Reason & H. Bradbury (Eds.), *Handbook of action research: Participative inquiry and practice* (pp. 91–102). Thousand Oaks, CA: Sage.

Kemmis, S., & McTaggart, R. (2005). Participatory action research: Communicative action and the public sphere. In N. K. Denzin & Y. S. Lincoln (Eds.), *The Sage handbook of qualitative research* (pp. 559–603). Thousand Oaks, CA: Sage.

Kemmis, S., & Wilkinson, M. (1998). PAR and the study of practice. In B. Atweh, S. Kemmis, & P. Weeks (Eds.), *Action research in practice: Partnerships for social justice* (pp. 21–36). New York: Routledge.

Khanlou, N., & Peter, E. (2005). Participatory action research: Considerations for ethical review. *Social Science & Medicine, 60,* 2333–2340.

Kidd, S., & Kral, M. (2005). Practicing participatory action research. *Journal of Counseling Psychology, 52*(2), 187–195.

Kincheloe, J. L. (2003). *Teachers as researchers: Qualitative inquiry as a path to empowerment* (2nd ed.). New York: Routledge.

Lewis, H. M. (2001). Participatory research and education for social change: Highlander Research and Education Center. In P. Reason & H. Bradbury (Eds.), *Handbook of action research: Participative inquiry and practice* (pp. 356–362). Thousand Oaks, CA: Sage.

Lincoln, Y., & Goulet, D. (1998). Commodity and paradigm. In O. Fals-Borda (Ed.), *People's participation: Challenges ahead* (pp. 227–231). NY: Apex Press.

Lundy, P., & McGovern, M. (2006). Participation, truth and partiality: Participatory action research, community-based truth-telling and post-conflict transition in Northern Ireland. *Sociology, 40*(1), 71–88.

Lykes, M. B. (1989). Dialogue with Guatemalan Indian women: Critical perspectives on constructing collaborative research. In R. Unger (Ed.), *Representations: Social constructions of gender* (pp. 167–185). Amityville, NY: Baywood Publishing.

Lykes, M. B. (1997). Activist participatory research among the Maya of Guatemala: Constructing meanings from situated knowledge. *Journal of Social Issues, 53*(4), 725–746.

Lykes, M. B. (2001). Creative arts and photography in participatory action research in Guatemala. In P. Reason & H. Bradbury (Eds.), *Handbook of action research: Participative inquiry and practice* (pp. 363–371). Thousand Oaks, CA: Sage.

Maglajlic, R. A. (2004). Right to know, UNICEF BiH—Developing a communication strategy for the prevention of HIV/AIDS among young people through participatory action research. *Child Care in Practice, 10*(2), 127–139.

Maguire, P. (1987). *Doing participatory research: A feminist approach.* Amherst: The Center for International Education, University of Massachusetts.

Maguire, P. (2004). Reclaiming the F-word: Emerging lessons from teaching feminist-informed action research. In M. Brydon-Miller, P. Maguire, & A. McIntyre (Eds.), *Traveling companions: Feminism, teaching, and action research* (pp. 117–135). Westport, CT: Praeger.

Marincowitz, G. J. O. (2003). How to use participatory action research in primary care. *Family Practice, 20*(5), 1–11.

Mbilinyi, M. (1982). The unity of struggles and research: The case of peasant women in West Bagamoyo, Tanzania. In M. Mies (Ed.), *Fighting on two fronts: Women's struggles and research* (pp. 102–142). The Hague: Institute of Social Sciences.

McDonald, J. P. (1992). *Teaching: Making sense of an uncertain craft.* New York: Teachers College Press.

McIntyre, A. (1997). *Making meaning of whiteness: Exploring racial identity with white teachers.* Albany: State University of New York Press.

McIntyre, A. (2000). *Inner-city kids: Adolescents confront life and violence in an urban community.* New York: New York University Press.

McIntyre, A. (2003). Participatory action research and urban education: Reshaping the teacher preparation process. *Equity and Excellence in Education, 36*(1), 28–39.

McIntyre, A. (2004). *Women in Belfast: How violence shapes identity.* Westport, CT: Greenwood Publishing Group.

McIntyre, A., & Lykes, M. B. (2004). Weaving words and pictures in/through feminist participatory action research. In M. Brydon-Miller, P. Maguire, & A. McIntyre (Eds.), *Traveling companions: Feminism, teaching, and action research* (pp. 58–77). Westport, CT: Praeger.

McTaggart, R. (1991). Principles of participatory action research. *Adult Educational Quarterly, 41*(3), 168–187.

McTaggart, R. (Ed.). (1997a). *Participatory action research: International contexts and consequences.* Albany: State University of New York Press.

McTaggart, R. (1997b). Guiding principles for participatory action research. In R. McTaggart (Ed.), *Participatory action research: International contexts and consequences* (pp. 25–43). Albany: State University of New York Press.

McTaggart, R. (2001). Guiding principles of participatory action research. In C. F. Conrad, J. G. Haworth, & L. R. Lattuca (Eds.), *Research in higher education: Expanding perspectives* (2nd ed., pp. 263–274). Boston: Pearson Custom Publishing.

Mduma, E. K. (1982). Appropriate technology for grain storage at Bwakira Chini village. In Y. Kassam & K. Mustafa (Eds.), *Participatory research: An emerging alternative in social science research* (pp. 198–213). New Delhi: Society for Participatory Research in Asia.

Mikkelsen, H. B. (2001). *Methods for development work and research: A guide for practitioners.* Thousand Oaks, CA: Sage.

Mills, G. (2006). *Action research: A guide for the teacher researcher* (3rd ed.). Upper Saddle River, NJ: Prentice Hall.

Minkler, M., & Wallerstein, N. (Eds.). (2003). *Community-based participatory research for health*. San Francisco: Jossey-Bass.

Morawski, J. G. (1994). *Practicing feminisms, reconstructing psychology: Notes on a liminal science*. Ann Arbor: University of Michigan Press.

Noffke, S. E., & Somekh, B. (2005). Action research. In B. Somekh & C. Lewin (Eds.), *Research methods in the social sciences* (pp. 89–96). Thousand Oaks, CA: Sage.

One STEP Group, McIntyre, A., & McKeirnan, P. (2000). *At a split second: Visual stories of/by young people living in an urban community*. Fairfield, CT: Fairfield University.

Preston-Whyte, E., & Dalrymple, L. (1996). Participation and action: Reflections on community-based AIDS intervention in South Africa. In K. De Koning & M. Martin (Eds.), *Participatory research in health: Issues and experiences* (pp. 108–110). London: Zed Books.

Reason, P. (1993). Sitting between appreciation and disappointment: A critique of the special edition of *Human Relations* on action research. *Human Relations, 46*(10), 1253–1270.

Reason, P., & Rowan, J. (Eds.). (1981). *Human inquiry: A sourcebook of new paradigm research*. Chichester, England: John Wiley & Sons.

Reinharz, S. (1992). *Feminist methods in social research*. New York: Oxford University Press.

Rocheleau, D., Ross, L., Morrobel, J., & Hernandez, R. (1998). Gendered landscapes, gendered lives in Zambrana-Chacuey, Dominican Republic. In I. Guijt & K. Shah (Eds.), *The myth of community: Gender issues in participatory development* (pp. 178–187). London: Intermediate Technology.

Schön, D. A. (1983). *The reflective practitioner*. New York: Basic Books.

Siu, K. W. M., & Kwok, J. Y. C. (2004). Collective and democratic creativity: Participatory research and design. *Korean Journal of Thinking and Problem Solving, 14*(1), 11–27.

Spaniol, S. (2005). "Learned hopefulness": An arts-based approach to participatory action research. *Art Therapy: Journal of the American Art Therapy Association, 22*(2), 86–91.

Stewart, A. J. (1994). Toward a feminist strategy for studying women's lives. In C. E. Franz & A. J. Stewart (Eds.), *Women creating lives: Identities, resilience and resistance* (pp. 11–36). Boulder, CO: Westview.

Swantz, M. (1982). Research as education for development: A Tanzanian case. In B. Hall, A. Gillette, & R. Tandon (Eds.), *Creating knowledge: A monopoly?* (pp. 113–126). New Delhi: Society for Participatory Research in Asia.

Tandon, R. (1981). Participatory research in the empowerment of people. *Convergence, 14*(3), 20–27.

Tandon, R. (1996). The historical roots and contemporary tendencies in participatory research: Implications for health care. In K. de Koning & M. Martin (Eds.), *Participatory research in health: Issues and experiences* (pp. 19–26). London: Zed Books.

Trimble, J. E., & Fisher, C. B. (Eds.). (2005). *Handbook of ethical considerations in conducting research with ethnocultural populations and communities.* Thousand Oaks, CA: Sage.

Tuan, Yi-Fu (1999). *Who am I? An autobiography of emotion, mind, and spirit.* Madison: University of Wisconsin Press.

Veroff, S. (2002). Participatory art research: Transcending barriers and creating knowledge and connection with young Inuit adults. *American Behavioral Scientist, 45*(8), 1273–1287.

Vio Grossi, F. (1980). The socio-political implications of participatory research. In F. Dubell, T. Erasmie, & J. de Vries (Eds.), *Research for the people—Research by the People: Selected papers from the International Forum on Participatory Research in Ljubljana, Yugoslavia* (pp. 69–80). Linkoping, Sweden: Linkoping University, and Amersfoort, The Netherlands: S. V. E. The Netherlands Study and Development Center for Adult Education.

Vio Grossi, F. (1982). Peasant participation, adult education, and agrarian reform in Chile. In B. Hall, A. Gillette, & R. Tandon (Eds.), *Creating knowledge: A monopoly?* (pp. 153–171). New Delhi: Society for Participatory Research in Asia.

Wade, R. C., & Anderson, J. B. (1996). Community service-learning: A strategy for preparing human service-oriented teachers. *Teacher Education Quarterly, 23*(4), 59–74.

Wadsworth, Y. (1984). *Do it yourself social research.* Melbourne: Victorian Council of Social Service and Melbourne Family Care Organization.

Wadsworth, Y. (1998). What is participatory action research? *Action Research International,* Paper 2. Retrieved from www.scu.edu.au/schools/gcm/ar/ari/p-ywadsworth98.html

Wadsworth, Y. (2001). The mirror, the magnifying glass, the compass and the map: Facilitating participatory action research. In P. Reason & H. Bradbury (Eds.), *Handbook of action research: Participative inquiry and practice* (pp. 420–432). Thousand Oaks, CA: Sage.

Wadsworth, Y. (2005). "Beloved Bangladesh": A Western glimpse of participatory action research and the animator-resource work of Research Initiatives Bangladesh. *Action Research 3*(4), 417–435.

Walton R. E., & Gaffney, M. E. (1989). Research, action, and participation: The merchant shipping case. *American Behavioral Scientist, 32*(5), 582–611.

Wang, C. C. (1999). Photovoice: A participatory action research strategy applied to women's health. *Journal of Women's Health, 8*(2), 185–192.

Wang, C., Wu, K., Zhan, W., & Carovano, K. (1998). Photovoice as a participatory health promotion strategy. *Health Promotion International, 13*(1), 75–86.

Whyte, W. F., Greenwood, D., & Lazes, P. (1989). Participatory action research: Through practice to science in social research. *American Behavioral Scientist, 32*(5), 513–551.

Wilkinson, S. (Ed.) (1996). *Feminist social psychologies: International perspectives.* London: Open University Press.

Women of ADMI & Lykes, M. B. (2000). *Voces e imágenes: Las mujeres Maya Ixiles de Chajul* [Voices and images: Mayan Ixil women of Chajul]. Guatemala: Magna Terra, and Washington, DC: EPICA.

Wu, K., Burris, M., Li, V., Wang, Y., Zhan, W., Xian, Y., et al. (Eds.). (1995). *Visual voices: 100 photographs of village China by the women of Yunnan Province.* Yunnan, China: Yunnan People's Publishing House.

Zeichner, K. (2001). Educational action research. In P. Reason & H. Bradbury (Eds.), *Handbook of action research: Participative inquiry and practice* (pp. 273–284). Thousand Oaks, CA: Sage.

Zeichner, K., & Melnick, S. (1996). The role of community field experiences in preparing teachers for cultural diversity. In K. M. Zeichner, S. Melnick, & M. L. Gomez (Eds.), *Currents of reform in preservice teacher education* (pp. 176–196). New York: Teachers College Press.

About the Author

Alice McIntyre is a professor and the director of elementary education at Hellenic College. She has conducted participatory action research for over a decade. She has authored three books and has co-edited another, all of which discuss PAR as an approach to engaging people in processes of reflection, education, and change. She is currently writing about a 2-year PAR project with 9- and 10-year-old Latina girls in the United States, focusing on what it means for them to be girls.